For Maids Who Brew & Bake

Rare & Excellent Recipes from 17th Century Newfoundland

Cover photo by Ned Pratt taken at the
Colony of Avalon, Ferryland, Newfoundland.

For Maids Who Brew & Bake

Rare & Excellent Recipes from 17th Century Newfoundland

by Sheilah Roberts

Flanker Press

2003

National Library of Canada Cataloguing in Publication

Roberts, Sheilah, 1954-
  For maids who brew & bake : rare & excellent recipes from 17th century Newfoundland / by Sheilah Roberts.

Includes bibliographical references.
ISBN 1-894463-46-3

  1. Cookery, Canadian--Newfoundland style. 2. Frontier and pioneer life-- Newfoundland and Labrador. I. Title.

TX715.6.R618 2003   641.59718   C2003-906140-X

Copyright © 2003 by Sheilah Roberts

Cover photo
NED PRATT

Layout and design
LILLIAN FIDLER DESIGN

PRINTED IN CANADA BY FRIESENS CORPORATION

FLANKER PRESS LTD.
P.O. BOX 2522, STATION C
ST. JOHN'S, NL
CANADA
A1C 6K1

TOLL FREE: 1-866-739-4420 TELEPHONE: (709) 739-4477 FAX: (709) 739-4420
INFO@FLANKERPRESS.COM   WWW.FLANKERPRESS.COM

Table of Contents

Introduction	1
Grains and Things	**7**
"It is fruitfull enough..."	7
"Nay if a man be at Sea..."	8
How to make Barley-broth	8
Brewis	9
Manners	9
"*How to bear yourself at table*"	9
Flumery	10
Renews	11
Vegetables and Salads	**13**
"We have also a plentifull Kitchin-Garden..."	13
Of Sallets simple and plain	13
Of the inward virtues... which ought to be in every housewife	14
Cupids	15
Carrots	17
"*How to bear yourself at table*"	17
To fry Garden-Beans	18
"*The summer time heere is so faire...*"	19
Pottage of parsnips	19
"*Use Mirth and good work...*"	20
A pottage with cabbage	20
Pottage of colliflowers	22
Peese-pottage	23
Fish	**25**
"May hath herings..."	25
Poore John fryed	27
"The inhabitants... build houses..."	27
"... the country is not the least improveable..."	28

v

Salmon stewed	28
Bonavista	29
"*Seeth them in equal parts water and ale,*"	29
Barnacle with short broath	29
"*Of the inward virtues...which ought to be in every housewife*"	30
Fresh cod broiled with ragoust	31
"*Fry your fish in oil...*"	32
How to stew a trout	32
"*The trout loves small Purling Brooks.*"	33
Poultry	**34**
April 16th, 1670 - Bay Bulls	34
To make a sallet of a cold Hen or Pullet	35
"*A Discourse of Dreams and their Interpretations.*"	36
To boyle a Capon or Chickin with Colle-flowres	38
"*How to bear yourself at table*"	39
An excellent broath	40
To season a chicken-pie	41
To boil Sparrows or Larkes	42
Ferryland	43
Egg Dishes	**48**
"*Our poultry have not onely laid Egges...*"	48
To fry an Egge as round as a ball	48
"*Bacon is good for carters and plowmen,*"	49
To make the best Tansie	49
The Legend of Sheila NaGeira	51
"*To all those worthy Women, who have any desire to live in Newfound-land*"	51
The best Pancake	52
"*[Let] no sort of women be suffred to goe thither but the Englishe...*"	54
To make the best panperdy	54
Harbour Grace	55
Meats and Game	**56**
"*Take your Pigg...*"	57

Sauce for a pig	58
To stew Beef in Gobbets, the French Fashion	58
"After meat taken..."	60
To make dumplings	61
Brigus	61
To make an Umble-Pye	62
"Neither are there any Snakes..."	63
To roast a gigot of Mutton	63
"Our high levels of land are adorned..."	64
To Stew Venison	65
"There is great store of deer..."	65
Frigasie of Rabbets	66
The Beothuk	67

Fruits and Flowers — 70

Berries growing in Newfoundland	70
"All manner of fruit..."	70
"Wife into thy garden, and set me a plot,"	71
To make conserve of Strawberries	71
An Amorous Dialogue between Thomas and Sarah.	72
Apples fried	73
The use of flowers	74
To make conserve of flowers	74
To make an excellent Tart-stuffe of Damsons	75
"To make all manner of fruit tarts."	76
How to make a Goosberry Fool	76
St. John's	77

Baking — 80

"The pudding is a dish very difficult to be described,"	81
To make a Raspberry Pudding	81
Port de Grave	83
To make Gingerbread	83
Women of the time	84
Minced Meat	86
Devonshire white pot	86

If you are watching your weight	87
To make leach of Almonds	88
"*Of the inward virtues...which ought to be in every housewife*"	89
To make Misers for Children to eat in Afternoons in Summer	90
Teenagers were a problem even then.	90
To make Hasty Pudding	91
Bay Bulls	92
A Pippen Pie	92
Bread Making	**94**
The receypte of the Dyett bread	96
"*Use a measure in eating...*"	96
Of baking manchets	97
"*How to bear yourself at table.*"	97
To make Spiced bread	98
To make bisket bread, otherwise called French bisket	99
Placentia	100
Drink	**103**
"But if you will make a right Gossips cup..."	104
Aqua Vitae	105
Rum	105
"*Of the inward virtues...which ought to be in every housewife*"	105
Spruce Beer	106
To make Hippocras	107
Torbay	108
The true bottling of Beere	108
"*That noe person doe set up any Taverne...*"	109
Wormwood wine	110
To make a syllabub	110
Miscellanea	**113**
How to draw your butter thicke	114
To make Clove or Cinnamon Sugar	115
How to hang your candles in the ayre without candlestickes	115
Cures	**117**
"*Fifteen Directions to preserve Health*"	117

Syrup of Turnips	120
"... exceeding good for scarby..."	120
A Recipe to help Digestion	121
For a Sore Throat	121
"Of the inward virtues...which ought to be in every housewife"	121
The lady Drury's Medicine for the cholick. Proved.	122
A Cordiall for wind in the stomack or any Part	122
"Great harms have come and maladies exceeding..."	123
To make the Face fair and for a stinking breath	123
For Heat in the Face, redness and shining of the nose	123
"Alwaies in your hands use eyther Corall or yellow Amber,"	123
For a cough	124
"In Winter time, warme well your garments..."	124
To stanch the bleeding of a Wound	124
A Bag to smell unto for Melancholy, or to cause one to sleep	125
"When you put off your garments to go to bed,"	125
For Pin, or Web, in the eye	125
To make Oil of Sage	126
For the Hearing	126
Of Sage flowers	126
King Edwards perfume to make your house smell like Rosemary	127
To cure corns	127
For Consumption	127
A letter from Cupids (John Guy 1611)	128
Against the trembling of the heart	128
To take away spots and freckles from the face or hands	128
Glossary	**133**
Acknowledgements	**135**
Sources	**137**
Bibliography	**145**

It may likewise please your honour to give expresse order that such be sent thither... Strong maids that (besides other worke) can both brew and bake.

*A request made by Captain Edward Wynne,
Governor of Ferryland in a letter to England.
Ferryland, August 17, 1622[1]*

Introduction

Sybil stood on deck and braced herself against the constant rolling and pitching of the ship. She clutched her woolen cloak tightly and looked up. High above, billowing white sails snapped in the wind and the shouts of sailors drifted over her. Land ahead. The other passengers were below deck where they'd spent most of the month-long voyage deep in the belly of the ship. As she scanned the clear blue line of the horizon, her excitement mounted. For a second, she shivered and letting go of her grasp on the gunnel, quickly pulled her hair, damp and sticky with sea salt, away from her face. She squinted into the wind, one last time, and then headed down below deck. What joy it would be to finally set foot on solid land again.

Our first settlers came from England and France, crossing an unforgiving Atlantic ocean, to settle in this strange and new-foundland. Maybe a desire for something different or a thirst for adventure brought them overseas and away from their homes. Perhaps they envisioned a new life full of opportunity for themselves and their children. In the seventeenth century wars and religious persecution raged throughout Europe. The Plague and the Great Fire ravaged London. Who could blame these people for wanting a change of scene? Life in the colonies, however, was no picnic, and sometimes the would-be settlers needed a little encouragement:

> The Iland of New-found-land is large, temperate and fruitefull, the fruitfulnesse of it consisting not only in things of sustenance for those that shall inhabit it, but in many sorts of comodities likewise, of good use and valew to be transported ... the Country of New-found-land ... is little inferior to any

₢ Introduction ₯

other for the commodities thereof; and lies, as it were, with open arms towards England, offering it selfe to be imbraced, and inhabited by us.

(Richard Whitbourne, 1620)[2]

Many of the new arrivals came from Dorset, Hampshire, Somerset and Devon. They settled on what was to be known as the English Shore, a section of land that stretched from Trepassey in the south, to Greenspond, Bonavista Bay, in the north. They built timber houses and made their homes in colonies that started up in the early 1600s. These early settlements were located at Cupids, Renews, Bristol's Hope and Ferryland. By 1675, there were over thirty inhabited sites on the island.

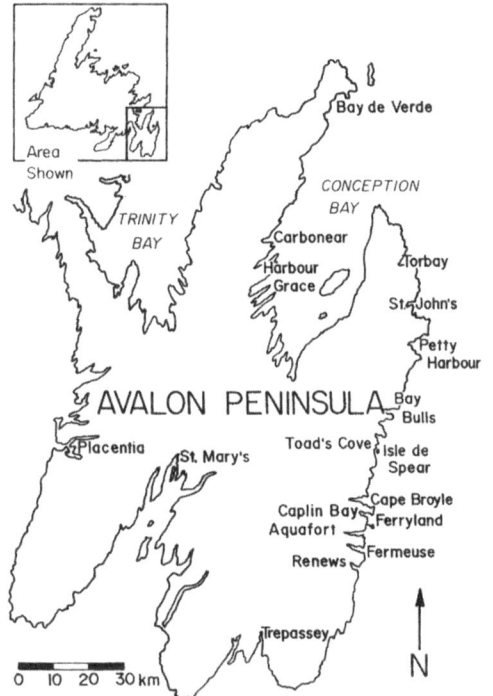

The Avalon Peninsula, with harbours and settlements of the south Avalon.
(The South Avalon Planters: 1630-1700, by Dr. P. Pope.)

⋘ Introduction ⋙

> The aire [is] subtle & wholesome, the Summer season pleasant conforme to the like latitude in Europe, saving that the woodie places in June & Julie are somewhat pestered with small Flies...
>
> (John Mason, 1620)[3]

The French on the island had their own settlements in Placentia, St. Mary's and on the south coast. Many of these people originated in the Basque regions of France.

The Spanish and Portuguese made no attempts at colonization, but continued to fish in the waters off the shores of Newfoundland.

When the new colonists arrived, they soon settled into the business of running their households. They set their kitchens up with dishes and hung cauldrons and kettles in large stone hearths. The hearth took up most of one wall and was the centre of family life. The housewife or maid got up well before sunrise each day and stirred up the coals from the night before to cook the first meal. Firewood was plentiful, so soon a good blaze warmed the early morning. Perhaps a cereal pottage bubbled in the large iron pot hung over the fire. On other mornings the table was laid with a simple fare of bread and ale.

Because it was the easiest way to prepare food, a lot of the cooking here in Newfoundland was probably cauldron cooking: the whole meal cooked in one pot. First the meat was put to boil in water, then the vegetables were placed in bags or nets and put in alongside; finally the pudding was spooned into a pudding bag and cooked along with everything else. Talk about efficiency! Sometimes meats were placed in earthenware cooking vessels, the tops sealed with pastry, and then put in the cauldron and cooked for hours.

If time permitted, the preferred method of cooking was roasting. You had to have a good cut of meat to do this, though, and someone always had to be on hand to turn the spit – a hot and time-consuming process. The meat was skewered on long iron spits, supported on

⋈ Introduction ⋈

spit dogs (iron stands) and roasted before the fire. Drippings from the meat were caught underneath in a "sauce pan," a long shallow pan with a sloping base that conducted the juice to a central well, where it could be taken up and used for basting. Other pots for cooking smaller amounts of food were called "pipkins" and made of iron, bronze, ceramic or tinned-copper. These pipkins were supported on trivets in front of the fire.

A "pipken" used for cooking small amounts of food.
(Courtesy of MUN Archaeology Unit.)

Bellows were used to keep the fire going, so it must have been a real art to maintain a constant temperature. The smoke from the fire went up the flue of course, but in the process also cured the bacon and ham hung there in niches.

When the meal was cooked, the whole family, including children, servants and workers, gathered around the "board" or table. In the early part of the century, food was still served on wooden trenchers, and cutlery consisted of knives and spoons.

∞ Introduction ∞

Forks were not yet in common use, but napkins, an important part of the table setting, took their place. Food was held with the napkin in one hand and cut with the knife in the other.

Much of what the settlers needed they imported and paid for with profits from the fishery. Archaeological finds of expensive ceramics show that the major planters lived well and indulged their good taste. (Pope, 1992). I think we can assume that these people fed their stomachs equally well.

Newfoundland lacked the deep rich soil of England, so large-scale agriculture would have been very difficult. The settlers had kitchen gardens on their properties, though, and grew fresh herbs and vegetables to supplement their diets. They started their gardens with seeds and roots brought from the old country.

The Kitchen garden at Ferryland.
(Courtesy of MUN Archaeology Unit.)

෬ Introduction ෭

Turnips

Scrape them, blanch them, and seeth them with water, butter and salt; after they are enough, put them in a dish with very fresh butter, and you may put in some mustard; serve with nutmegg.[4]

The recipes I have chosen for this book come from old English manuscripts and reflect what might have been eaten by families in Newfoundland at that time. I have written "translations" with more useable quantities for many of the recipes, but have always included the originals with their rather unique turns of phrase, punctuation and spelling. The herbs used in my recipes are in most cases dried or powdered, but fresh herbs may be substituted. (Use 1 tbsp. of fresh for each 1/3 tsp. of powdered or each ½ tsp. of crushed.) Excerpts from the old manuscripts are full of words no longer in use today, and some words in this book are specific to Newfoundland. I have defined the unfamiliar ones in a small glossary.

Grains & Things

The smell of wood smoke fills the air as grey dawn approaches. By now our housewife has the cereal pottage ready. Usually a breakfast dish, it could be eaten at other meals as well. Pottage was common to all classes until the late seventeenth century. Wealthier families often added meat to it.

In the early days, the grain for our pottage would have been imported, although there were some who reported success growing it locally.

> It is fruitfull enough both of Sommer and Winter corne... wheate, rye, Barlie, oates and pease which have growen and ripened there as well and as timely as in Yorkshire in England.
>
> (John Mason, Newfoundland 1620)[5]

English Man-of-War.

Grains & Things

Grains were popular on long sea voyages.

> Nay, if a man be at Sea in any long Travel he cannot eat a more wholesome and pleasant meal than these whole Groats, boiled in water till they burst and then mixed with Butter and so eaten with Spoons, which although Seamen call simply by the name Loblolly, yet there is not any meat how significant soever the name be, that is more toothsome or wholsome.
>
> (Gervase Markham, 1656)[6]

Elizabeth Cromwell wrote the following recipe in her cookbook. Her note at the end of the recipe states that "this mess" was prepared frequently for her husband, Oliver.

How to make Barley-broth

> Take Barley and put in fair water, give it three qualms over the fire, separate the waters, and put it into a cullender, boyl it in a fourth water, with a blende of mace and a clove, and when it is boyled away, put in some raisons and currants, and when the fruit is boyled enough, take it off and season it with white [wine] rose-water, butter and sugar and a couple of yolks of eggs beaten with it.[7]

This makes a nice light meal at any time.

▼ ▼ ▼

1 cup of barley
enough water for cooking barley – about 3 cups or more
½ cup of raisins and/or currants
½ cup of white wine
2 tsp. of rosewater

¼ tsp. of cloves and mace blended
1 tsp. sugar
1 tbsp. butter
1-2 egg yolks (optional)

Soak the barley in water overnight and when ready to cook, drain and rinse. Cook in a pot with fresh water and simmer for 40-60 minutes, or until done. Strain off any excess liquid. Add remaining ingredients, mix in the beaten egg if desired, and serve.

Brewis

Brewis in the seventeenth century was made by crumbling bread into a bowl of boiling water and fat. Today we make brewis from hard bread or "hardtack," as it is known here. Newfoundlanders eat their brewis with salt fish in "fish and brewis" or with fresh fish in "fisherman's brewis." Some eat it with butter and sugar. The combination of the sugar on the brewis and the salt in the fish is quite delicious.

Manners were sometimes rather curious. Both men and women thought nothing of spitting. In one instance Samuel Pepys, the renowned English diarist of the 1600s, described an incident at a theatre in London.

> And here I was sitting behind in a dark place, [in the theatre], a lady spat backward upon me by mistake, not seeing me. But after seeing her to be a very pretty lady, I was not troubled at all.
>
> (Jan. 28, 1661)[8]

Many of the table manners, except for the spitting, were similar to what we know today.

Remove the spoon from the dish when you have taken up the food.

> Don't spit over the table, nor down upon it ever.
> Be it forbidden to put the elbow on the table.
> If you can, I warn (?) you of this, don't belch at table.
> At table do not mention how dear (expensive) things are.
> Don't say a word to any one which may be unpleasant to him.
>
> ("How to bear yourself at table")[9]

Flumery was fine oatmeal steeped a long time in water, strained and then boiled and stirred until it was almost solid. Here's how it was made.

Flumery

> From this small Oat-meal by oft steeping it in water and cleasing it, and then boyling it to a thick and stiff jelly is made that excellent dish of meat which is so esteemed of in the West parts of this Kingdom, which they call Wash-brew, and in Cheshire and Lancashire they call it Flamery, or Flumery, the wholsomeness and rare goodness, nay, the very Physick helps thereof, being such and so many, that I my self have heard a very reverend and worthily renowned Physician speak more in the commendations of that Meat, than of any other food whatsoever... Now for the manner of eating this meat... some eat it with Honey, which is reputed the best Sauce, some with Wine, either Sack, Claret or White; some with strong beer or strong Ale, and some with milk, as your ability or the accomodations of the place will administer.[10]

Other seventeenth century dishes.

The Duke of Hamilton

Charles I

The Duke of Hamilton, Sir David Kirke, and their associates were granted the entire island of Newfoundland in 1637 by King Charles I.

Renews

Mussel shells and barnacles cling to the seaweeds that cascade over the wet rocks on the shores of Renews. This rough-looking vegetation was possibly where the name Renews came from. The French word "rougnouse" means scabby or mangy. The name is first used in 1536 by Cartier and again in 1544 by Cordyer of Rouen.

Migratory fishermen visited the harbour here in the sixteenth century and cured their fish on the beach. During the seventeenth century there were several attempts to start colonies in the area. Among them was one in 1618 by Sir William Vaughan's men, and one in 1623 by Henry Cary. Sir William was a Welsh poet, visionary and adventurer who sent colonists to Newfoundland. He had dreams of a new Wales and called his colony Cambril Colchos. He sent his people first to Aquafort and in 1618, with newly appointed governor Captain Richard Whitbourne, moved them to Renews. These colonists, known by Whitbourne as the "Welsh Fools," were ill prepared for the way of life here and soon gave up and went home to Wales. Renews gathered more inhabitants after that, and a local folk tradition tells of the *Mayflower*'s visit to the port in 1620 to pick up supplies on its way to Plymouth Rock. In 1623 Lord Falkland (Henry Cary) brought over the first group of Irish settlers to the area. Some of the residents of Renews named in the 1675 census were Hooper, Cotton, Pooley, Hudley, Lane and Davis.

Uncovering a planter's house in Renews.
(Courtesy of MUN Archaeology Unit.)

Vegetables & Salads

Kitchen gardens have always been a common sight in Newfoundland outports, their broad-leaved greens and climbing beans and peas neatly kept and fenced in, to keep out wandering animals. Many of the men and women who came as settlers were skilled gardeners and grew a variety of produce in their small plots. No doubt they made good use of the plentiful supply of local fertilizer: fish offal and lime-rich sea-shells.

> We have also a plentifull Kitchin-Garden and so ranke, that I have not seene the like in England..." Our Beanes are exceeding good: our Pease shall goe without compare; for they are in some places as high as a man of an extraordinary stature; Raddish as big as mine arme; Lettice, Cale or Cabbedge, Turneps, Carrets and all the rest is of like goodnesse.
>
> (Capt. Wynne, Governor of Ferryland, in a letter dated August 17, 1622)[11]

Other vegetables likely grown here were broad beans, cauliflower, leeks, onions and parsnips – perfect for the making of "sallet" or salad as we now know it.

Of Sallets simple and plain

> First then to speak of Sallets, there be some simple, some compounded, some only to furnish out the Table, and some both for use and adornation; your simple Sallets are Chibols pilled, washt clean: and half of the green tops cut clean away, and so served in a fruit dish, or Chives, Scallions, Rhaddish roots,

☙ Vegetables & Salads ❧

boyled Carrots, Skirrets, and Turnips, with such like served up simply; Also all your Lettuce, Cabbage-lettuce, Purslane, and divers other herbs which may be served simply without any thing but a little Vinegar, Sallet Oyl and Sugar: Onions boyled and stript from their rind and served up with Vinegar, Oyl and Pepper is a good simple Sallet: so is Camphire, Bean-cods, Sparagus, and Cucumbers, served in Likewise with Oyl, Vinegar and Pepper, with a world of others, too tedious to nominate.[12]

Ferryland vegetables. (Courtesy of Colony of Avalon Foundation.)

Of the inward virtues...
which ought to be in every housewife

Most of the cookbook authors of that day were men. One well-known author, Gervase Markham, began his book *The English Housewife* with a description of what he thought was the ideal woman.

ଅ Vegetables & Salads ଓ

Let her dyet be wholesom and cleanly, prepared at due hours, and cook'd with care and diligence: let it be rather to satisfie nature then her affections and apter to kill hunger than revive new appetites; let it proceed more from the provision of her own yard, than the furniture of the Markets, and let it be rather esteemed for the familiar acquaintance she hath with it, than for the strangeness and rarity it bringeth from other countries.[13]

Translation: Make sure the meals are on the table on time. Don't burn anything and let there be enough of it to fill me up. Instead of spending my good money at a market, grow it yourself. Don't feed me anything strange. Just give me good plain food that I'm used to.

Cupids

Cupids is the oldest permanent European settlement in Newfoundland and the first British colony in what was to become Canada.

The harbour is long and sheltered and reaches deep inland. Located at the bottom of Conception Bay, not far from Brigus, this colony of "Cuper's Cove" was sponsored by the newly formed Company of Adventurers and Planters of the City of London and Bristol in 1610. John Guy was in charge, and in that year he brought with him to the island, thirty-nine colonists along with his brother Philip, nine goats, a boar, two pigs, poultry, cunnies (rabbits) and pigeons. The colony started with just a few houses. Eventually they added a sawmill, storehouse, gristmill and a stockade armed with three cannon. After two mild winters, Guy convinced sixteen women to come out and join the colony, and they were soon followed by even more settlers. The new settlement was not without its problems. A pirate named Peter Easton terrorized them in 1612 and Guy estimated that Easton stole up to £20,000 worth of goods. A setback for sure, but they persevered and on March 27, 1613 the first English child was born in Newfoundland to Nicholas Guy and his wife.

∽ Vegetables & Salads ∾

Cupids archaeological site.
(Courtesy of Baccalieu Trail Heritage Corp, Inc.)

Vegetables & Salads

Carrots

Cleanse and seeth them; when they are sod, peel them, and cut them into very thin round slices, frie them with fresh Butter, and onion minced, salt, pepper, and vinegar; then serve.[14]

Carrots came in several colours in those days, either purple, yellow or white. The white ones were used as cattle feed. Try this recipe with whatever colour carrot you can find.

▼ ▼ ▼

4-5 carrots, peeled
1 medium onion, minced
butter or olive oil for frying
2 tbsp. of red wine vinegar

Boil the carrots as you normally would and then take them off the heat and cut them into thin round slices or sticks. Melt the butter (or heat the oil) in the pan on a medium-low heat. Add the minced onion and fry only until translucent. Do not brown. Add your carrot pieces and the wine vinegar. Toss to coat. Serve as an accompaniment to any meal.

At table be cheerful, and don't speak to any one in his ear.
Let not a cat ever be a companion to you at the table.
If you are wise spit beyond the vessel when you wash.
Carefully beware of this, not to offend your fellow guests.
Never grin, but sit steady, with three clean fingers touching the food.
("How to bear yourself at table")[15]

◌ℬ Vegetables & Salads ℬ◌

To fry Garden-Beans

Boil them and blanch them and fry them in sweet Butter,
with Parsly and shred onions, and a little Salt;
then melt butter for the sauce.[16]

▼ ▼ ▼

2 cups of fresh or frozen green beans cut into pieces.
1 medium onion, minced fine
2 tbsp. of dried parsley or ½ cup of fresh
salt to taste
butter for frying

Boil the beans for several minutes until tender crisp and then drain. Fry the onions and parsley in butter and, when the onions become translucent, add the beans and salt to taste. Sauté for several minutes, and if desired add a little more butter for a sauce.

Morris dancers.

ଓଗ Vegetables & Salads ଅଠ

The Summer time heere is so faire, so warme, and of so good a temperature, that it produceth many herbes and plants very wholesome, medicinable and delectable, many fruit trees of sundry kinds, many sorts of Berries wholesome to eate, and in measure most abundant; in so much as many sorts of birds and beasts are relieved with them in time of Winter.

(Captaine Edward Wynne – Governor of Ferryland August 17, 1622.)[17]

Pottage of parsnips

Clense them well, and chuse the middle sized ones, seeth them with butter and a bundle of herbs and season them with salt, and clove sticked, then take them out, & take off the skin if you will, and then put them with butter, and a drip of Broath; stove them, and you shal find your sauce thickened; your bread being also well soaked, and your potage filled, garnish it with your Parsnips, then serve.[18]

▼ ▼ ▼

5-6 medium sized parsnips
3 tbsp. of butter or oil
1 tsp. rosemary
2 tbsp. parsley
½ tsp. thyme
½ tsp. ground cloves
¼ tsp. of salt
1 cup of chicken broth

Cut the peeled parsnips in rounds and fry in the butter for 10 minutes until golden brown. Add the herbs and spices and fry a few more minutes. Pour on the broth and cook for a further 15-20 minutes or until parsnips are tender and liquid is reduced.

Use Mirth and good work
At bed and at board.
Provide for thy husband, to make him good cheer,
Make merry together, while time ye be here.
At Bed and at board, howsoever befall
Whatever God sendeth, be merry withall.
(Thomas Tusser, 1577)[19]

A pottage with cabbage

Make a good strong broath with mace, and cloves, a little of each: three or foure oynions, a bunch of sweet herbes: boyle all these with meatt in water till it be pretty strong; then strayne of and set it over the fire, then take the crust of 2 or 3 french loves well dryed and stoved over coals with some of the Broath; then melt a little butter in a sawce-pan and slice in an oynion; then have a ladlefull of cabbage cleane drayned and boyled tender, give it two or three chops with a knife and flower it, let the sliced oynion be fryed till it change couller, but not browne, Take the third part of a pounde of french barly; boyle it very tender in three waters, then drayne the water from it and when it is cold put it to a quart of creame, and a blade of mace, a nutmeg quartered, and a race of ginger cut into peeces; set it one the fire and let it boyle a prety while stil stirring it, season it with suger to your tast, then beat the yolks of foure eggs with a little of the creame, and mix them to the rest and let it boyle a little after the eggs are in; then have some twenty almonds blanched and beaten with some rose-water to keepe them from oyleing; then with a little of ye thynest of the firmity rub them through a strayner into your firmity; set it one the fire no more after ye almonds are in it; pick out the spice and stir in a little salt and sliced nutmeg to serve it.[20]

Full of vitamin C, this dish can be eaten as a main meal or served as a side dish.

▼ ▼ ▼

1 small head of cabbage shredded or chopped
2 tbsp. of flour
3 onions sliced thin
1 cup of cooked barley
1/8 tsp. each of mace, cloves, nutmeg and ginger
½ tsp. of thyme
1 tbsp. dried parsley
2 cups of meat or vegetable stock
¼ cup of ground almonds
2 tsp. of rosewater
1 tsp. sugar
1 cup of cream
A pinch of saffron (optional)

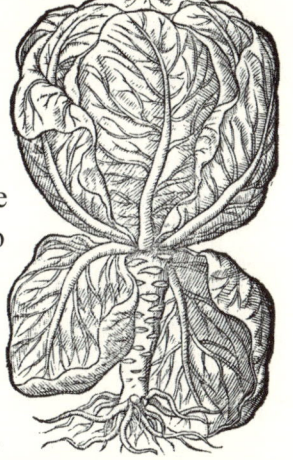

If saffron was not available, the dried centres of marigolds were used as a substitute.

Have the barley cooked and ready and then combine the shredded cabbage and flour. Place in a large pot and toss to coat. Add all the other ingredients except the cream and bring to a boil. Reduce heat and simmer for about 20-30 minutes. When the cabbage is tender pour in cream and simmer for another 5 minutes on medium-low heat. Egg yolks may be used as a thickener if desired. Garnish with parsley.

Pottage of colliflowers

Fit your Coliflowers as for to put them with butter, and blanch them but very little, then make an end of seething them, and season them well; soak your bread with any broth you have, and garnish it with your Coliflowers fryed in butter, salt, and nutmegge, and besprinkle them with almond broth, then serve.[21]

This is a nice side dish to accompany fish or chicken.

▼ ▼ ▼

1 head of cauliflower, broken into florets
2 tbsp. of butter or oil
¼ tsp. or more of nutmeg
½ cup of chicken or vegetable broth
¼ cup of ground almonds
salt and pepper to taste

Blanche the florets for 3 minutes in boiling water and then remove and drain. Melt the butter in a large frying pan and add the florets. Fry for 2-3 minutes then pour on the broth. Cover and let it simmer for 3 more minutes. Sprinkle with the ground almonds and adjust seasoning if necessary.

Pease pottage was considered the national dish of Tudor and Stuart England. It was usually boiled along with bacon or pickled pork. In Newfoundland it is still cooked with the traditional Jiggs dinner and known as pease pudding.

⌘ Vegetables & Salads ⌘

Peese-pottage, My Lady Howe's Receipt

Take some of your best yellow peese, boyle them and bruse them, and strayne them out: then put them in a pott and boyle them with a good great peece of butter and some sweet herbes, and an oynion stuffed with cloves, and a little mace: shread some capers and put in, and when it boyles cutt the bottoms and tops of french manchets and tost them lay them in the dish and so serve it.[22]

Yellow split peas seem to be able to absorb all the salt you can throw at them. No wonder it was such a popular side dish with the preserved meats. It is best to salt this dish after it is cooked.

▼ ▼ ▼

1 cup of yellow split peas
4 cups stock or water
2 tbsp. parsley
1 tsp. thyme
1 tsp. rosemary

"Boyle them with a good great piece of Butter." - North Devon butter pots.
(Courtesy of MUN Archaeology Unit.)

Vegetables & Salads

one onion stuffed with cloves
¼ tsp. of mace.
1 tbsp. of capers, minced (optional)
salt to taste
¼ cup of butter

Soak the peas overnight in water and discard any that float. Drain them and then place the peas, along with the herbs, spices and onion into a pudding bag. Place this in a pot with the hot water or stock. Bring to the boil and simmer for about 45 minutes or until the peas are soft. Remove the bag and empty the peas out into a bowl. Remove the onion and serve as a side dish if you like. Add the butter to the peas and beat until they are creamy. Add salt to taste.

☙ Section ❧

Fish

When John Mason wrote home to England in 1620, he was amazed at the size and quantity of fish found here on the island.

> May hath herings one equall to 2 of ours, cants and cod in good quantity. June hath Capline a fish much resembling smeltes in forme and eating and such aboundance dry on shoare as to lade cartes, in some partes pretty store of Salmond, and cods so thicke by the shoare that we nearlie have been able to rowe a boate through them. Julie and so till November hath Macrill in aboundance one thereof as great as two of ours. August hath great large Cods but not in such aboundance as the smaller, which continueth, with some little decreasing until December.[23]

There was a high demand for fish in seventeenth century Europe, and, as a result, the fishery off the coast of Newfoundland flourished. Fish caught here were shipped to France, Italy, Portugal and Spain – Catholic countries that lacked good fishing grounds close to home. Dry cod was popular in these regions because it kept well in hot weather and church law dictated that good Christians had to eat fish on Fridays and during Lent. The West Country merchants in England made a handsome profit from this trade and loaded their returning ships with luxury goods such as wine, olive oil and raisins. Some of these goods made their way back to Newfoundland when the ships returned to engage in the fishery.

The Newfoundland fishery was carried out from small boats, where the fishermen caught their cod using hand lines with baited hooks. They brought them ashore, cut their heads off, gutted them and removed the backbone. When the fishery started, usually in June, the

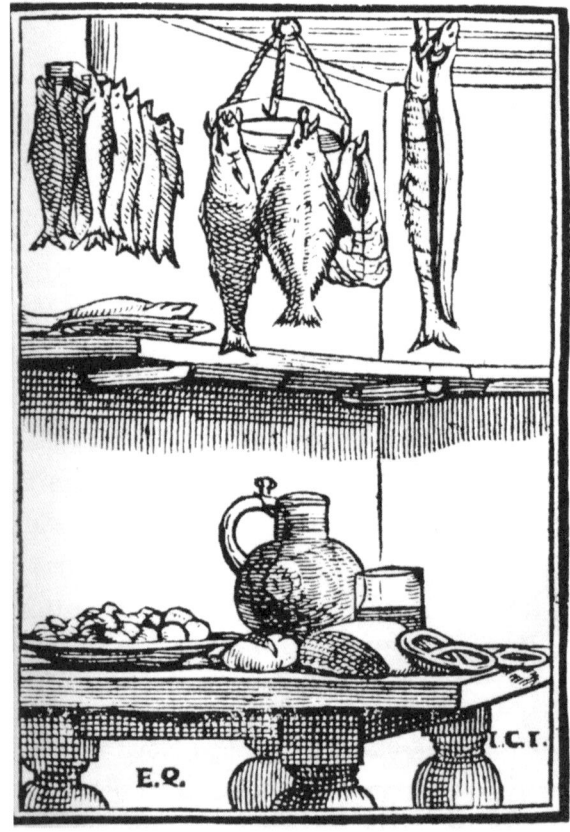

men worked eighteen to twenty hours a day until the fish stopped by mid or late August. The fish caught were either salted and stored immediately on boats for transportation back to Europe, or they were salted and dried on flakes for an extended period of time. This dried fish has always been an important part of our maritime diet. My mother cooked it the same way my ancestors did, soaking it first in water to remove the salt, and then boiling it. We ate it plain with potatoes, brewis and scrunchions (bits of fried pork fat). In the seventeenth century the settlers probably ate it with mustard, butter or vinegar.

⊰ Fish ⊱

Poore John fryed

After it is well watered, cut it into peeces and seeth it, after it is sod drain it, and fry it with butter, onion, peper, nutmegg, and vinegar then serve.[24]

To make dry fish, also called "Poor John" or "Stock Fish," you needed a good piece of shore with fresh water and woods near by. This piece of shore was called a "fishing room," and prime real estate like this was in high demand. There was lots of competition amongst the newly arrived vessels for the best spots, and rivalry developed between the settlers and the visiting fishermen for access to these parts of the shore. An Englishman by the name of William Hinton wrote of St. John's in 1670,

> The inhabitants ... build houses and make gardens and orchards in places fitt for cureing and drying fish, which is a great hinderance and not to be suffered.
>
> (Hinton, 1670)[25]

This echoed the views of the West Country merchants who were not in favour of colonization and sought to uproot the settlers. They claimed that the settlers debauched the fishermen with rum and bad women. They also had little good to say about the physical environment, even though it is somewhat accurate.

Fish

"... the country is not the least improveable whereby to give subsistance to ye inhabitants, it being nothing but woods, boggs and rockes."[26]

Some other species of fish available on the island were trout, salmon, halibut, mackerel, herring, capelin and eels. Seventeenth century families ate these fish either stewed, stuffed and baked, or tied to spits between wooden lathes and roasted. Smaller fish could be broiled on a gridiron or fried in butter. Fish were served on "sops" (slices of toast) with warm melted butter poured over them. Because the potato had not yet come into general use, most of their dishes were served on bread or bread soaked in broth.

Salmon Stewed

Cut it into slices of the thicknesse of two or three fingers, and put it after the way of stewing, sticked with cloaves in a kettle with white or red wine, well seasoned with butter salt and minced onyon, seeth it well with capers if you have any, when the sauce is short and thickened, serve, and garnish with what you will.[27]

That was quite the size of a salmon steak! Perhaps we could start with something a little more modest.

▼ ▼ ▼

4 salmon steaks ¾ to 1 inch in thickness
40 cloves (10 each). Add more or less according to taste.
2-3 tbsp. of butter
1 medium onion thinly sliced
½-1 cup of white wine
salt

Melt the butter in a frying pan. Sauté the onion slices until clear. Stick the salmon steaks with cloves, add them to the pan and sprinkle with salt. Fry on medium low heat about 3 minutes per side or until almost done. Add the wine and cover the pan, cooking for a further 2-3 minutes on low heat.

Bonavista

By 1677 Bonavista was the second most populous town on the island. The 1677 census shows residents with surnames like Newell, Shambler, Warrey, Wallis, Phippard, Wiry, Kates [Keats?], Curtiss, Crew, Newman, Tilley, Gickery, Brent, Gantlett and Talbott.

James Shambler was one of the wealthier settlers. He employed twenty-two men and had eight head of cattle, twenty-eight sheep and fifty-one pigs.

Seventeenth century families were fond of shellfish and ate lots of mussels, periwinkles, lobsters, crabs, shrimps and prawns. A favourite way to cook shrimp was to "seeth them in equal parts water and ale, salt and savoury." (Gervase Markham, 1656)

Here's one for barnacles, if you're brave.

Barnicle with short broath

> Dreste and lard it, then seeth it with water, and season it well, when it is half sod, put to it a quarte of white wine, and seeth it well, then serve it with parsley over it.[28]

Mr. Markham had this to say about how a housewife should dress.

> Let therefore the Housewifes garments be comely and strong, made as well to preserve the health as adorn the person, altogether without toyish garnishes, or the gloss of light colours and as far from the vanity of new and fantastick fashions, as neer to the comely imitations of modest matrons.[29]

Fish

Fresh cod broiled with ragoust

After it is dressed, you must butter it, and broile it on the gridiron, seasoned with salt and clove sticked; as it is broiling, bast it with butter; after it is broyled, make a sauce with very fresh butter, into which, after it is halfe browne, you shall put some minced parsley, and if you will, some onyon or chibol, which you may take out, for such as are fantasticall, mix a little broth with it, a drop of vinegar and minced capers; soake your cod in its sauce; when you are ready to serve, put some mustard in to it, if you will, then serve.[30]

▼ ▼ ▼

1 lb (454 kg.) of cod fillet
cloves to stick into the fish
1 large onion
2-4 tbsp. of butter or olive oil
2 tbsp. of fresh parsley or one of dried
2 tsp. of red wine vinegar
¼ cup broth (chicken or vegetable)
minced capers (optional)

Salt cod fillet to taste and stick it with cloves. Lay it on a flat pan and grill at 400°F for about 5-10 minutes depending on the thickness of your fish. Meanwhile melt some of the butter in a frying pan, put in parsley and onion and fry until onions are soft. Add the wine vinegar and broth to the pan and simmer for a few minutes. Use this as a sauce for the fish. If you are feeling really "fantasticall," garnish it with the capers.

In 1611 Sir Hugh Platt in his book *Delights for Ladies to adorne their persons, tables, closets and distillories* suggested:

Fry your fish in oil, some commend rape oil and some the sweetest Seville oil that you can get, for the fish will not taste at all of the oil because it hath a waterish body and oil and water make no true unity, then put your fish in white wine vinegar, and so you may keep it for the use of your table at any reasonable time.[31]

How to stew a trout

Take a large Trout, fair trimm'd, and wash it, and put it into a deep pewter dish, then take half a pint of sweet Wine, with a lump of butter, & a little whole Mace, Parsley, Savory & thyme, mince them all small, and put them into the Trouts belly, and so let it stew a quarter of an hour: then mince the yelk of an hard egg, and strew it on the Trout, and, laying the Herbs about it, and scraping on Sugar serve it up.[32]

▼ ▼ ▼

1 lb. trout, cleaned and gutted
2 tbsp. butter
a dash of mace
4 tbsp. of fresh parsley
½ tsp. of dried savoury
½ tsp. thyme
½ cup of white wine
1 hard boiled egg yolk
salt to taste

Place the fish in a pan. Knead the herbs into the butter, and spread in the cavity or on the fish. Add white wine, cover the dish and let stew for 15 minutes. Remove from the pot and sprinkle with minced egg yolk and salt.

The trout loves small Purling Brooks, or Rivers that are very swift, and run upon Stones, or Gravel; he feeds while he is in strength in the swiftest Streams, behind a Stone, Log, or some small bank that shooteth into the River, and ther lyes watching for what comes down the Stream. He spawns about October.

(H. Woolley, 1686)[33]

ஓ Section ஐ

Poultry

April 16th. Having stayed in Bay Bulls all this time, living a jolly life, with Mr. Richd. Munyon; Rd. Avent, Caleb Hall and Mr. Hingston, all chyrurgeons of Plymouth and in our mutual carousing spent all our liquor and good things designed for the whole voyage.

(James Yonge, Newfoundland 1670)[34]

In a Stuart banquet many different dishes adorned the table. Poultry dishes would most certainly have been among them.

Preparing to roast a chicken on the spit.

To make a sallet of a cold Hen or Pullet

Take a Hen and roast it, let it be cold, carve up the legs take the flesh and mince it small, shred a lemmon, a little parsley and onyons, an apple a little pepper and salt with oyl and vinegar, garnish the dish with the bones and lemmon peel, and so serve it.[35]

Perhaps the bone garnish was a way of letting the guest know the identity of the beast being consumed, a signpost of sorts.

▼ ▼ ▼

2 cups of diced, cooked poultry
1 cup diced apple
¼ cup diced red onion
¼ cup fresh parsley
1 tbsp. finely grated lemon peel

Dressing:

⅛ cup red wine vinegar
⅜ cup of olive oil
1 tsp. of sugar
salt and pepper to taste

Combine the poultry, apple, red onion and parsley in a dish. Sprinkle on the lemon peel and toss. Mix up the salad dressing in a covered container and shake well. Pour on the dressing, to taste, just before serving.

"Sallets" included both hot and cold salads seasoned with oil and vinegar dressings. A "salmagundi" was a mixed salad with meat added to it. This became known as a Solomongundy.

By the seventeenth century it was known that lemons and limes cured scurvy, and the medical people of the day suggested going to sea with enough of the citrus fruits on board to ward off the disease. The shipping owners were too cheap, however, and continued to "victual" their ships with cheap bulky food which consisted of sour beer, hard ships biscuit (full of weevils and a good source of protein) and rancid cheese "as tough as old leather." Bon apetit!

If all that good food has made you sleepy, perhaps a short nap is in order. And if you sleep, perchance to dream, this is what your dreams might mean.

A Discourse of Dreams and their Interpretations

To Dream you see white Hens upon a Dunghill, signifies Disgrace by some false accusation.

To dream one is in a pleasant Meadow, signifies the possession of Riches, and the advantage of pleasure.

To dream one fights and overcomes, is to have the advantage over ones Adversary in Law Suits or otherwise.

To dream it Thunders and Lightens, is a figure of approaching sickness.

To dream two Lovers meet and have not power to speak to each other, denotes the match will be broken off by means of their Parents.

To Dream you see Death in sickness, and that he flies you is a sign of recovery.

To dream of kisses and Embraces signifies suddain Marriages.

To dream you are dead and laid out, signifies a dressing for the Nuptials.

To dream of gay Cloathing, and that upon your back they turn to rags, signifieth poverty.

To dream one is with Child and knows not the Father, denotes her Marriage with a stranger.

To dream one sees the Sun in it's brightness, signifies the favour of Great ones.

To dream a Ring drops off ones Finger denoteth a disapointment in Love.

To dream one has a Garland of Flowers brought and presented, denotes he or she will have the Party desired.

(*The Art of courtship; or the school of delight*, 1686)[36]

Seventeenth century couples.

Poultry

To boyle a Capon or Chickin with Colle-flowres

Out of the budds of your flowres, boile them in milke with a little Mace, till they be very tender: then take the yolkes of two eggs straine, them with a quarter of a pint of Sacke then take as much thicke butter being drawne with a little vinegar and a sliced Lemmon, and brue them together, then take the flowers out of the milk and put them into the Butter and Sacke, then dish up your Capon being tender boyld, upon Sippets, strowing a little salt on it, and so poure on the sawce upon it and so serve it to the Table hotte.[37]

The sherry and drawn butter give this dish a rich and unusual taste.

▼ ▼ ▼

1 boiled or baked chicken
½ cup of drawn butter (see recipe on page 114)
½ cup of sherry
2 beaten egg yolks (optional)
1-2 tbsp. of lemon juice

Cauliflower

2 cups of milk
1 medium sized cauliflower
¼ tsp. of mace
salt and pepper to taste

While the chicken is cooking, prepare the drawn butter. Add the sherry and egg yolks (if you wish to thicken the sauce) to the drawn butter and stir on low heat until mixture thickens.

Bring the milk, nutmeg and cauliflower to a boil and turn down the heat. Simmer until the cauliflower is tender, and season to taste. Remove cauliflower from the milk and place around the cooked chicken. Pour the drawn butter sauce over each serving of chicken and cauliflower. The remaining milk can be used as a soup base.

◌ Poultry ◌

The table manners of the day are somewhat amusing by today's standards.

> Let not the piece of food, when it has been touched by the teeth, be put back Upon the dish. Let your fingers and nails be trimmed.
>
> Let not the salt be touched by meat in the vessel in which it is set on table.
>
> While food still continues in your mouth, beware of drinking.
>
> Don't scratch your limb, after the fashion of a mole, as you sit down.
>
> Let not persons eating, clean their teeth with their knife.
>
> ("How to bear yourself at table")[38]

A dinner scene.

An excellent broath

Take a Chicken and set it on the fire, and when it boils scum it, then put in a Mace and a very little Oatmeal, and such herbs as the party requires, and boil it well down and bruise the Chicken and put it in again and it is good broath: and to alter it you may put in six Prunes, and leave out the herbs or put them in as you please, and when it is well boyled, strain it and season it.[39]

I am not sure why they bruised the chicken, perhaps to get all the goodness out of the bones, or perhaps to tenderize it. Unlike the chickens of today these fowl probably had muscles.

▼ ▼ ▼

1 chicken cut in pieces
6 cups of water
1 onion chopped
1 tbsp. of parsley
1 tsp. of thyme
1 tsp. of savoury
½ cup or more of oatmeal
6 prunes
1 tsp. of salt or to taste

Boil the chicken until tender, about 45-60 minutes. Remove the pieces and use for the chicken pie if desired, or de-bone and return to the soup pot. Add the rest of the ingredients and simmer for another 30 minutes. As you serve it, be sure to include a prune or two at the bottom of each bowl. Your guests will get a pleasant surprise as they finish their soup.

ଔ Poultry ଓ

To season a chicken-pie

Having your Paste rolled thin, and laid in your Baking-pan, lay in some butter; then lay in your Chickens quartered, and seasoned with Pepper, Nutmeg, and a little Salt, then put in Raisins, Currans and Dates, then lay butter on the top, close it, and bake it, then cut it up and put in clouted ream, Sack and Sugar.[40]

▼ ▼ ▼

2 large chicken breasts or several chicken pieces about 1 lb. de-boned
1 tbsp. of currants
1 tbsp. or raisins
¼ cup of dates
1 tin of thick cream - 170 ml (approximately ¾ cup)
½ cup of chicken broth
2-4 tbsp. of sherry
salt and pepper to taste
¼ tsp. of nutmeg
prepared puff pastry

Boil the chicken pieces for about 45 minutes or until done. Take the meat off the bones and chop into cubes. Add the rest of the ingredients to the meat and place in a pie dish. Cover with puff pastry and bake at 400°F for 25-30 minutes. Frozen puff pastry is convenient and can be used to cover the pie. Follow the directions for baking on the package.

Now in case you're in the mood for something a little different...

❧ Poultry ☙

In the kitchen.

To boile Sparrows or Larkes

Take two ladles full of Mutton broth, a little whole Mace: put into it a peece of sweet Butter, a handfull of Parsley, being picked; season it with Sugar, Verjuice, and a little Pepper.[41]

They give no instructions for adding the birds, but I guess they relied on the common sense of the housewife.

Hunting.

Poultry

Ferryland

On the rolling downs of Ferryland, you can sense the spirit of times gone by. The grassland lies like a thin blanket over ancient rock that stretches down to the sea, and the waves still pound the shores as they did when the first colonists came over.

The name Ferryland probably came from the Portuguese "farelhão", which meant small headland. George Calvert, or Lord Baltimore as he was to be known later on, received a land grant from James I to start a colony at Ferryland. He named this colony "Avalon" after the Avalon in Somersetshire, England, where Christianity was believed to have started. This Colony of Avalon was a large section of land which stretched across the southern shore of what is now the Avalon Peninsula. It was Captain Edward Wynne, who along with eleven other Welshmen, began to build the colony in 1621. He wrote letters back to England describing their progress.

> As soone as the house and fortification is fitted and finished I shall (God willing) prepare and fence in a proportion of seede ground and a Garden close by the house. It may please your Honour not to send any Cattle the next yeere, because I cannot provide fodder for them so soone, before there bee some quantity of Corn [grain] growing, but it may please your honour to send some Goats, a few tame Conies [rabbits] for breedeing, as also Pigs, Geese, Ducks and Hens. I have some Hens already: some spades from London were necessary, if of the best making also some good Pick-axes, iron croes, and a Smith... [42]

The task must have been daunting, but they continued on.

> Notwithstanding our diligent labour & extraordinary paines-taking, it was All hallowtide before our

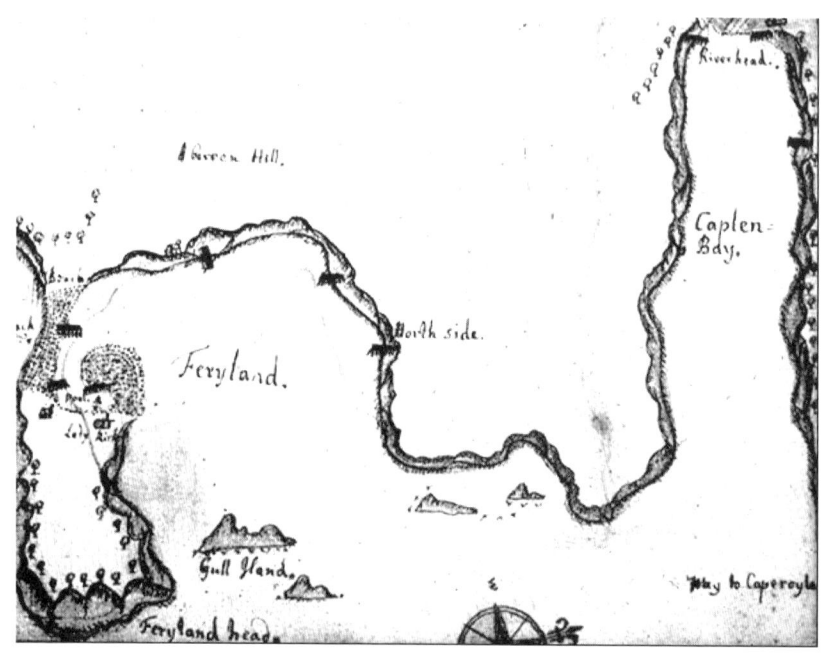

The harbour of Ferryland

first range of building was fitted for an habitable being...a hall 18 foot long and entry of 6 foot, and a cellar of 20 foot in length, and of the height betweene the ground floore and that over head about 8 foote, being devided above, that throughout into four chambers, and four foot high to the roofe or a halfe storie....our kitchin, of length 18 foot, 12 foot breadth, and 8. foot high to the eves, and walled up with stone-work with a large Chimney in the frame...

And there was still more to come.

For addition of building we have at this present a Parlour of fourteene foote besides the chimney, and twelve foot broad, of convenient height, and a lodging chamber over it; to each a chimney of stone-worke with staires and a staire-case, besides a tenement of two roomes, or a storie and a halfe, which serves for a store house till wee are otherwise provided. The Forge hath been finished this five weekes: the Salt-worke is now almost ready.

(Ferryland, 1622)[43]

George Calvert finally came to visit in 1627. He must have liked it because he returned to England and brought back his wife and some of his children. Lord Baltimore himself was a Catholic, but he saw the colony as a place for religious tolerance. Unfortunately he fell out with an Anglican clergyman living there, a certain Erasmus Stouton, who went back to England and complained bitterly to the king. This, along with the horrible winter Baltimore and his family experienced in that year of 1628-29, had a profound effect. He wrote back to England, "It is not to be expressed with my pen what wee have endured." Shortly after that, he applied for land in Virginia.

David Kirke was next in line to take over at Ferryland, and take over he did. He levied heavy taxes on the settlers and the summer fishermen and amassed a fortune. Kirke lived in great comfort in Baltimore's Ferryland "mansion" from 1638 until 1651 when the king called him back to London to account for his activities in Ferryland. A trial was held and the court took statements from the residents. Two of the women who testified shed an interesting light on his character! The examiners asked the women how well they knew him and Phillip(a) Davis replied, "a little too well and she wisheth she had not known him."

Amie Taylor said: "she loves Sir David Kirke best." (testimony taken in Newfoundland in 1652)[44]

David Kirke never returned to Newfoundland and died in 1654, imprisoned in England. He was accused by the second Lord Baltimore

The waterfront at Ferryland. (Painting by David Webber).

of having illegally taken over the plantation of Avalon and was awaiting trial. Because of his death, the matter was never resolved, and his wife, Lady Sarah, took over the plantation. Sarah and the rest of the Kirke family stayed in Ferryland and continued to prosper.

The French invaded Ferryland in September of 1696 and ransacked the settlement. They took the residents and transported them to Renews to be shipped back to England. The prisoners were taken in small boats out to the ships. For one English woman it must have been all too much, for she jumped over the side of the shallop into the waves of the cold Atlantic ocean and drowned herself.

☙ Poultry ❧

Archaeologists have found animal remains at Ferryland in the Colony of Avalon which include rabbit, chicken, duck, geese, sheep, pig, cow, seal, caribou, horse, rat and bird, along with lots of fish bones.

They certainly had a varied diet! (I'm hoping the rats were just spectators.)

Lord Baltimore

Section

Egg Dishes

Our poultry have not onely laid egges plentifully, but there are eighteen young chickens, that are a week old, besides others that are a hatching.

(John Guy in a letter from Cupids 1611)[45]

Eggs were an important source of protein in the early days. Because chickens were easy to keep, even a poor family could keep one or two. Eggs were used as a thickening agent in many dishes or eaten on their own. They were not eaten in Lent or on Fridays, and this practice carried on until the middle of the seventeenth century. Traditionally the yolks were for the lords and the whites for the commoners, and in many recipes of the time the whites of the eggs are often discarded. Whites were considered "viscous and cold, and slackens the digestion and doth not engender good health." In Newfoundland, the colonists ate chicken, duck, goose and seabird eggs. These could be roasted in the embers, poached or fried in lard. Poached eggs were considered best for your health, and fried eggs the worst.

To fry an egge as round as a ball

Take a broad posnet or a deepe frying-panne and a quart or three pints of clarified butter or sweete Suet heate it as hot as you doe to fry Fritters then take a sticke and stirre it till it run round like unto a whirley-pit, then breake an egge into the middle of the whirle and turne it round with our sticke until it bee as hard as soft pocht egge, and the whirling of your suet will make it as round as a bal, then take it up with a slice and put it into a warme pipkin and set it leaning against the fire, for so you may doe as many as you please, and they will keepe hot halfe an hour at the least and yet be soft.[46]

This sounds a bit dangerous, but no doubt the cooks of those days were highly skilled. I wonder how many houses burned down because the cook was trying to round out an egg?

Eggs were often eaten with thin strips of bacon called "collops." Hence, the humble beginnings of the bacon and egg breakfast.

> Bacon is good for carters and plowmen, the whiche be ever labourynge in the earth or dunge... wherefore I do say that coloppes and egges is as holsome for them, as a talowe candell is good for a horse mouth or a peese of powdred beef is good for a blereyed mare. (Andrew Boorde, 1542)[47]

To make the best Tansie

> First, then for making the best Tansie, you shall take a certain number of Eggs, according to the bigness of your Frying-pan, and break them into a dish, abating ever the white of every third Egge: then with a spoon you shall cleanse away the little white Chicken knots, which stick unto the yolks; then with a little Cream beat them exceedingly together: then take a green Wheat Blades, Violet leaves, Strawberry leaves, Spinage, and Succory, of each a like quantity, and a few Walnut tree buds:

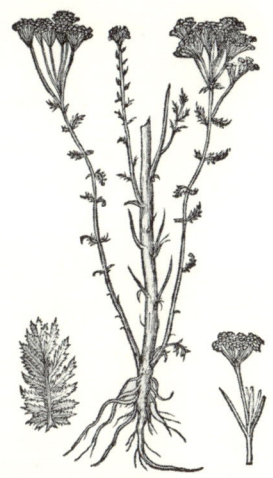

ଓଃ Egg Dishes ଃଠ

chop and beat all these very well, and then strain out the juyce and mixing it with a little more Cream, put it on the Eggs, and stir all well together, then put in a few Crums of bread, fine grated, Cinnamon, Nutmeg, and salt: then put some sweet Butter into the Frying-pan, and so soon as it is dissolved or melted, put in the Tansey and fry it brown without burning and with a dish turn it in the pan as occasion shall serve; then serve it up having strewed good store of Sugar upon it, for to put in sugar before will make it heavey.[48]

Tansy is a bitter herb that was popular in medieval times and up through the seventeenth century. Several types of this plant grow in Newfoundland. If you don't feel like going into the fields to gather some, try this:

▼ ▼ ▼

½-1 cup cooked spinach
¼ cup light cream
2 eggs plus 1 egg yolk at room temperature
⅔ cup fine bread crumbs
⅛ tsp. each of cinnamon and nutmeg
salt to taste
1 tbsp. of oil or butter for frying

Drain and chop the spinach well. Beat the eggs and cream together. Combine all ingredients. Heat the oil or butter until quite hot and then pour mixture into pan and reduce heat immediately. Turn when set, and brown on the other side.

Perhaps the most colourful legend from seventeenth century Newfoundland is the one of the "Irish princess" Sheila NaGeira. Kidnaped by a Dutch warship while she was on her way to school in France, she was rescued by an English ship captained by Peter Easton, a soon to be pirate. She fell in love with a member of the ship's crew, a young officer by the name of Gilbert Pike, and the two of them went ashore at the colony of Bristol's Hope in Newfoundland. It was there that she spent her life and raised a family. She is reputed to have lived to the ripe old age of 105.

The settlers wanted women on the island to keep homes and start families. In 1621 Edward Wynne, the man in charge of the early Ferryland colony, showed that he was definitely in favour of having women here when he said, "Women would bee necessary heere for many respects."

Another gentleman by the name of Robert Hayman, the governor at Bristol's Hope, near Carbonear, resorted to poetry to entice the fairer sex over to Newfoundland.

To all those worthy Women, who have any desire to live in Newfound-Land

Sweet creatures, did you truely understand
The pleasant life you'd live in Newfound-land,
You would with teares desire to be brought thither:
I wish you, when you goe, faire wind, faire weather:
For if you with the passage can dispence,
When you are there, I know you'll ne'r come thence. [49]

Was this a polite way of saying that once they made that sometimes awful sea voyage, they would probably never want to set foot on a sailing vessel ever again? Who knows.

ॐ Egg Dishes ॐ

A seventeenth century lady.

In any case, his "ad" was answered, and women came to marry the Newfoundland planters and fishermen.

The best pancake

To make the best Pancake, take two or three Eggs, and break them into a dish, and beat them well: then add unto them a pretty quantity of fair running water, and beat all well together; then put in Cloves, Mace, Cinnamon, and Nutmeg, and season it with Salt: which done, make it thick as you think good with fine wheat Flour; then fry the cakes as thin as may be with sweet Butter, or sweet seam, and make them brown, and so serve them up with Sugar strewed upon them. there be some which mix pancakes with new milk or cream, but that makes them tough, cloying, and not crisp, pleasant and savoury as running water.[50]

▼ ▼ ▼

2 eggs
¼ tsp. each of mace, cloves and nutmeg
½ tsp. cinnamon
¼ tsp. salt
1 cup flour
1 ½ cups of water
butter or oil for frying

Sift together the dry ingredients. Beat in the eggs and add enough water to make a thin batter. Heat the pan very hot, then turn it down to medium to fry the cakes. These pancakes are more like our modern crepe, so follow the instructions and "fry the cakes as thin as may be." In Newfoundland, pancakes were often eaten with molasses.

It seems that some wanted only women of a certain "quality" to settle on the island. In Lord Falkland's instructions to his settlers he wrote:

> [Let] noe sort of women be suffred to goe thither but the Englishe & such as have hade good educacion in Englande which will make a good nation in tyme for those will maintaine the language to ther Children & then it is noe great matter of wha[t] nation the men bee soe the women bee Englishe.[51]

To make the best panperdy [Pain Perdu]

> To make the best Panperdy, Take a dozen Eggs, and break them, and beat them very well, then put unto them Cloves, Mace, Cinnamon, Nutmeg, and a good store of Sugar, with as much Salt as shall season it: then take a Manchet, and cut it into thick slices like Toasts; which done, take your Frying pan, and put into it good store of sweet butter, and being melted, lay in your slices of bread, then pour upon them one half of your Eggs; then when that is fried, with a dish turn your slices of bread upward, and then pour on them the other half of your Eggs, and so turn them till both sides be brown; then dish it up and serve it with Sugar strewed upon it.[52]

The skillet that this dish was cooked in probably had short legs to enable it to sit over the coals of a fire. In the days of Oliver Cromwell, cookware was not only useful but educational as well. Pieces were decorated with mottos like "The wages of Sin are death" and "Pity the Poor." If you were so inclined, you could consider the weighty issues of morality as you cooked.

Egg Dishes

Harbour Grace

Harbour Grace is situated on the western side of Conception Bay. People from the Channel Islands came here to fish in the earliest days of the fishery, and by the seventeenth century many had settled in the area.

Harbour Grace was first known as Havre de Grace, and the area around it and north to Carbonear was called Bristol's Hope. Some of the settlers from John Guy's colony at Cupids came up here to make their homes. In 1622, Richard Whitbourne reported that the colonists "builded there faire houses, and done many good services, who live there very pleasantly." Close by was Carbonear, which by 1675 had the third largest population in Newfoundland. When the French attacked in 1697, two hundred settlers took refuge on Carbonear Island and successfully defended it against the invaders.

The Snows from Devon owned property in Harbour Grace, and in the 1677 census some other Harbour Grace surnames were Horton, Hibbs, Hanlon, Player, Batten, Taylor, Green and Palmer.

Thomas Hanlon was a wealthy citizen in Harbour Grace. He had two boats, nine employees, ten head of cattle and nine pigs.

Section

Meats & Game

The smell of the roasting joint filled the house, and fat sizzled as it dripped off the meat into the pan below. Wiping the sweat from her brow, the housewife turned the spit a little more before she tended to the small pot on a trivet nearby. To ensure the meat was browned evenly on all sides, constant turning of the spit was necessary.

The meat might also be put to boil in a large cauldron hung from a rod that stretched over the fire. This method needed little tending and left the cook free to attend to other duties.

Seventeenth century families ate their meat either fresh or preserved. Because it was usually quite tough and gristly, boiling was one of the better ways to cook it. They boiled the meat in water and

Meats & Game

seasonings and served it either in its own broth or on a plate with vegetables, saving the broth as a soup base for later use.

The housewife preserved meat by drying or smoking, by soaking in brine or in vinegar pickle, or by dry-salting. Preserved meats boiled up with vegetables were a staple maritime meal in the winter and spring. These meats had to be soaked or "watered" first to get rid of the large amounts of salt used in their preservation. They often shared the pot with things like oatmeal, dried peas, beans, bread crumbs or whole grains. These grains and legumes absorbed a lot of the salt and also worked as a thickener.

Vegetables used in cooking preserved meat, were cut fine in the earlier part of the century and were used more for seasoning than for accompaniment. Later on, the vegetables became side dishes. Now known as "Jiggs' dinner" or "corned beef and cabbage," this is still a traditional meal. What we call "corned beef" in Newfoundland is actually "naval beef" – what the Royal Navy packed in casks and put on board their ships to victual the crews on long ocean voyages.

The pickling process could preserve meat for a short time. If it was to be preserved for a long time, perhaps all winter, it was "soused" in a stronger solution. In Newfoundland if you are drunk you are sometimes referred to as being "pickled" and if you are really drunk, then you are "soused."

In the early part of the century, the settlers imported meat from England and Ireland, but eventually they kept their own livestock: herds of cows, sheep, pigs and chickens. Pigs were popular because they were easy to feed. Here are some instructions from an Englishman, Thomas Newington, on how to kill a pig:

Take your Pigg and hold the head down a payle of cold water until strangeled, then hang him up buy the heals and fley him, then open him, then chine him down the back as you do a porker first cuting of his head, then cut him in fower quarters.53

Sauce for a pig

To make sauce for a Pig, some take Sage and roast it in the belly of the Pig, then, boiling Verjuice, Butter and Currants together take and chop the sage small, and mincing the brains of the Pig with it put all together and so serve it up.54

Perhaps we could leave the brains out of it.

Another popular dish of the time was stew or "hotpot." It used up the rougher cuts of meat. Here is a delicious example of a hotpot in the "French fashion."

To stew Beef in Gobbets, the French Fashion

Take a flank of Beef, or any part but the Leg, cut it into slices, or Gobbets as big as Pullets-Eggs, with some Gobbets of Fat, and boyl it in a Pot or Pipkin with some fair Spring-water, scum it clean, and after it hath boyled an hour, put to it Carrots, Parsnips, Turnips, great Onions, some Salt, Cloves, Mace, and whole

Pepper; cover it close, and stew it, till it be very tender; and half an hour before its ready put into it some pick'd Thyme, Parsley, Winter-savoury, Sweet marjoram, sorrel, and Spinage (being a little bruised with the back of a Ladle) with some Claret-Wine: then Dish it on fine Sippets, and serve it to the Table hot; Garnish it with Grapes, Barberris or Gooseberries.[55]

▼ ▼ ▼

1 large onion, chopped
1 lb. of stewing beef cut in cubes
1 tsp. savoury
½ tsp. each of thyme and marjoram
¼ tsp. each of mace and cloves
2 tbsp. of fresh parsley, minced
1 cup of red wine
2 parsnips
3 carrots
½ a large turnip or one small one
1 cup of cooked spinach (optional)
add salt and pepper to taste

Fry the onions in a little vegetable oil and then add the meat to brown. Place your herbs, spices and ½ cup of the wine in a pot and bring to the boil. Reduce heat and simmer for 1-2 hours or until very tender. Add vegetables and the remaining wine and cook for another 45 minutes or until vegetables are done. Add more wine or water if necessary. Season to taste.

This stew may be thickened with flour and water if desired or with the traditional breadcrumbs. The added spinach is nice, but some may take exception to "green" things in their stew. Even in the early recipes, many of the green herbs were considered optional.

᛫ Meats & Game ᛫

After meat taken, neither labour in body nor mind must be used, and wash the face and mouth with cold water, clense the teeth either with Ivory, or a Harts horne, or some picker of pure silver or gold. After your banquets, passe an houre or two in pleasant talkes, or walke yee very gently and soberly, neither use much watchings long in the night, but the space of two howres goe to your bed; but if honest businesse doe require you to watch, then sleepe afterwards so much the longer, that your sleepe may well recompence your former watchings.

(Sir John Harington, 1624)[56]

To make dumplings

Season flour with salt, pepper and yeast, let your water be more than warm then make them up like manchets but let them be somewhat little, then put them into your water when it boileth and let them boil an hour, then butter them.[57]

Bellarmine jug found at Cupids – used for decanting liquor.
(Courtesy of Baccalieu Trail Heritage Corp., Inc.)

Brigus

The village of Brigus still has a quaint old-English feel to it. Located to the west of the capital of St. John's, Brigus lies nestled in the hills of Conception Bay not far from Cupids.

⚜ Meats & Game ⚜

There is a folk tradition which says that the Spracklin family purchased "half the harbour of Brigus" from John Guy in about 1612. In 1677, there were three main families, six house servants and forty-three fishing servants living there. The population grew steadily from then on and the town was a "considerable settlement" by the time the French came to burn it down in 1697.

To make an Umble-Pye.

Lay Beef-suet minc'd in the bottom of the Pye, or slices of Inter-lardede Bacon and cut the Umbles as big as small Dice, cut your Bacon in the same Form, and season it with Nutmeg, Pepper, and Salt, fill your Pyes with it, with slices of Bacon and Butter, close it up, and bake it; Liquor it with Claret, Butter, and stripped Thyme, and so serve it.[58]

In this recipe they have taken the humble "umble" and elevated it to greater heights. Umble pies were always baked fresh after the slaughter because the umbles did not keep well.

▼ ▼ ▼

1 lb of beef liver cut in small cubes
4 slices of bacon cut in small pieces
1 tsp. of nutmeg
½ tsp. thyme
½ cup of red wine
salt and pepper

Put liver and bacon in a baking dish and add nutmeg, pepper and salt. Cover and bake in a 325°F oven for about 30 minutes. Add the wine and thyme, then reheat and serve. If desired, cover with a pastry crust, increase heat to 375°F, and bake a further 10-12 minutes or until crust is golden brown.

Neither are there any Snakes, Toads, Serpents or any other venemous Wormes, that ever were knowne to hurt any man in that Countrey, but onely a little nimble Fly, (the least of all other Flies) which is called a Muskeito; those Flies seeme to have a great power and authority upon all loytering and idle people that come to the New-found-land.

(Richard Whitbourne, 1620)[59]

To roast a gigot of mutton

To roast a gigot of mutton, which is the leg splatted, and half part of the loin together; you shall, after it is washed, stop it with cloves, so spit it, and lay it to the fire, and tend it well with basting: then you shall take vinegar, butter, and currants, and set them on the fire in a dish or pipkin; then when it boils you shall put in sweet herbs finely chopped, with the yolk of a couple of eggs, and so let them boil together; then the meat being half roasted you shall pare off some part of the leanest and brownest, with sugar, cinnamon, ginger, and salt, and so put it into a clean dish: then draw the gigot of mutton and lay it on the sauce, and throw salt on the top, and so serve it up.[60]

To make the sauce, use:

▼ ▼ ▼

1 cup of water
1 tbsp. of sugar
3 tsp. of vinegar
2 tbsp. butter
1 tsp. of mint
1 tsp. of rosemary

Meats & Game

½ tsp. of fennel, ground
½ tsp. of cinnamon
½ tsp. of ginger
6 tbsp. of currants
2 beaten egg yolks

Take a leg of lamb or lamb chops and cut slits in the meat to insert the cloves and bake as you would normally. Combine all ingredients, except the currants and egg yolks. Bring to the boil and then simmer for 5 minutes. Add the currants. Remove from heat and let cool a bit. Beat in egg yolks and return to the boil, stirring constantly until thickened. Serve with the lamb.

Our high levels of Land are adorned with Woods, both faire and seemely to behold, and greene all Winter. Within land there are Plaines innumerable, amany of them containing many thousand Acres, very pleasant to see to, and well furnished with Ponds, Brookes and Rivers, very plentifull of sundry sorts of fish, besides store of Deere, and other beasts that yeeld both food and furre.

(John Guy, 1611).[61]

Meats & Game

To Stew Venison

If you have much Venison, and do make many cold baked Meats, you may stew a dish in hast thus: When it is sliced out of your Pye, Pot, or Pasty, put it in your stewing-Dish, and set it on a heap of coals, with a little Claret Wine, a sprigg or two of Rosemary, half a dozen Cloves, a little grated bread, Sugar, and Vinegar, so let it stew together a while, then grate on Nutmeg, and Dish it up.[62]

This recipe is also wonderful with stewing beef.

▼ ▼ ▼

3 tbsp. butter or olive oil
2 pounds venison or beef, cut into 1 inch cubes
¼ cup flour
1 cup red wine
1 tsp. rosemary
⅛ tsp. ground cloves
¼ cup of brown sugar
¼ cup vinegar
½ tsp. of salt
½ cup bread crumbs (optional)

Melt butter or oil in a saucepan. Dredge meat cubes in flour and brown in melted butter or oil in a cast-iron baking pot if possible. Combine wine, herbs and spices, vinegar, sugar and salt. Pour this liquid over the meat. Cover and simmer for 2 hours or until meat is tender. If more liquid is needed, add wine, water or stock. Add bread crumbs to thicken if desired.

There is great store of deer [caribou], whereof they saw some divers times, and twice they came within shot of them; and the greyhound, who is lustie, had a course, but could not get upon them. But nearer unto Cape Razo, [Cape Race], Reneuse, and Trepasse there is a great quantitie of open graound and stagges.

(John Guy in a letter to Master Slaney, 1611)[63]

Frigasie of Rabbits

Cut your Rabbits in small pieces, and mince an handful of thyme and parslie together, and with a Nutmeg, Pepper and Salt, season your Rabbits; then take two eggs and verjuice beaten together, then throw it in the pan, stick it, and dish it up on sippets.[64]

This recipe is delicious when used with chicken or rabbit.

▼ ▼ ▼

2 lbs. of tender, young rabbit or chicken pieces (skinned)
½ cup of water
¼ tsp. of nutmeg
½ tsp. of thyme
1 tbsp. of dried parsley
1 tbsp. of lemon juice
1 egg

Brown the rabbit (chicken) pieces in a little oil or butter. Pour in ½ cup of water, herbs and nutmeg. Cover tightly and simmer for 30 minutes. Remove the pieces from the pot. Beat a small amount of the hot broth into the beaten egg and lemon juice mixture and then whisk this into the remaining broth. Cook until thickened. Serve this sauce over the rabbit or chicken.

The Beothuk

There are few records left behind about the contact that must have occurred between the early settlers and the native Beothuk Indians. Here is one charming record of how John Guy met them on his voyage of discovery around Trinity Bay in 1612.

Mr. Whittington and Frances Tipton went ashore and encouraged the natives to come over. They did, and...

> ...then all fower togeather daunced, laughing & makeing signes of joy & gladnes, sometimes strikeing the breaste of our companie and sometymes theyre owne.[65]

An impromptu picnic followed. The natives brought meat from their canoes and then John Guy and Mr. Teage...

> presented them with a shirte, two table napkins & a hand towell, giving them bread, butter and reasons of

the sun to eate & beere & aquavitae to drinke and one of them blowing in the aquavitae bottle yt made a sound which they fell all into a laughture at.⁶⁶

The Beothuks ate caribou meat and hunted seals, whales and porpoises. They also fished, collected shellfish and seabird eggs, and hunted wild birds. In summer, they picked berries and edible roots.

They [the Beothuk] ate Deeres flesh dried in the smoke or Windes...and pulled up a root washed it and after dividing it among the foure [John Guy's crew], it tasted very well.

(John Guy's account of a voyage around Trinity Bay).⁶⁷

No doubt the settlers observed some of the natives and learned from them how to adapt to the new environment. Food preservation techniques for this new world were important skills to learn.

We opened a pack of venison. The Indians had preserv'd Forty or Fifty packs by the frost. We found in the wigwam all the Bones of the Deer was taken out

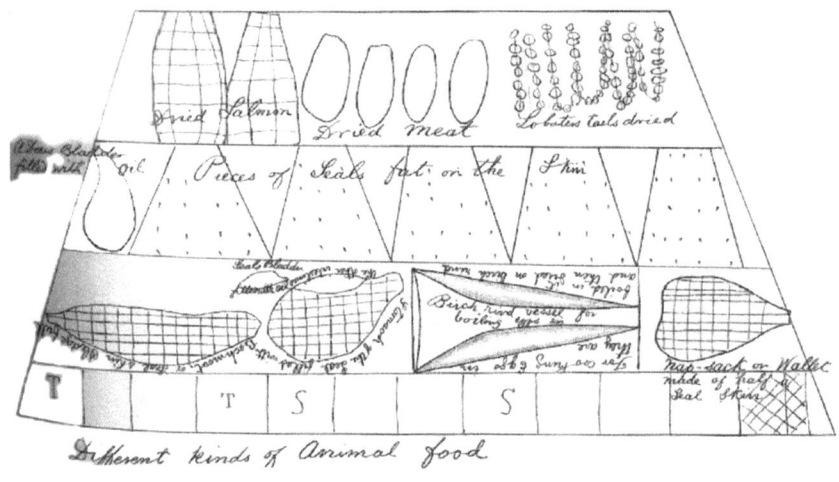

Meats & Game

and the Flesh press'd together in packs nearly square of four or five the longest way.

(George Pulling, 1792)[68]

The Beothuk cached meat and food in large storehouses, and once frost set in, the meat froze solid and remained unspoilt for weeks or months. They made caribou fat into clear grease and rendered oil from seal blubber. Salmon, caribou and probably berries and roots were dried by the fire to preserve them. The native people ate sculpins that were split like codfish. They made dishes and pots of birch rind and cooked their food using the "pot boiler" technique – scalding hot rocks were dropped into the "pots" to keep the water boiling and cook the food.

[We] happened to come suddenly where they had set up three Tents, and were feasting, having three such Cannowes by them, and three Pots made of such rinds of trees, standing each of them on three stones, boyling, with twelve Fowles in each of them, every Fowle as big as a Widgeon, and some so big as a Ducke: they had also many such pots so sewed, and fashioned like leather Buckets... and those were full of the yolkes of Egges, that they had taken and boyled hard and so dryed small as it had been powder-Sugar, which the Savages used in their Broth, as Sugar is often used in some meates.

(Richard Whitbourne, 1620)[69]

⋘ Section ⋙

Fruits & Flowers

The third course at a Stuart dinner usually consisted of wine, fruit tarts, marmalades, preserves, suckets (a type of fruit juice) and jellies. A dinner with three courses like this was referred to as a "banquet," and probably only happened on special occasions. To make these special treats, the ladies of the household worked all though the summer gathering and "conserving" fruits for the rest of the year. Berries growing in Newfoundland included:

> a small pleasant fruite called a Peare ... excellent Straberries, and Hartleberries [blueberries] with aboundance of Rasberries and Gooseberries somewhat better than ours in England.
>
> (John Mason, 1620)[70]

In old England, they rarely ate uncooked fruit. By the seventeenth century it was still regarded with great suspicion and thought to be responsible for causing illness.

> All manner of fruit generally fill the blood with water, which boileth up in the body as new wine doth in the vessel, and preparteth and causeth the blood to putrefy, and consequently bringeth in sickness
>
> (Thomas Cogan, 1584)[71]

Strawberry plant.

Wife into thy garden, and set me a plot,
with strawberry roots, of the best to be got:
Such growing abroad, among thorns in the wood,
well chosen and picked, prove excellent good.

(Thomas Tusser, 1577)[72]

To make conserve of Strawberries

First seethe them in water, and then cast away the water, and straine them: then boile them in white wine, and worke as before in Damsons; or else straine them, being ripe: then boile them in Wine and Sugar till they be stiffe.[73]

This is a jam with character!

▼ ▼ ▼

2-3 cups of strawberries fresh (sliced) or frozen (thawed)
½ cup brown sugar
¼ cup of white wine

Combine the ingredients in a saucepan and bring slowly to the boil. Stir constantly until it boils, then turn the heat to medium low and let it simmer for about 30 minutes or until it thickens. Fresh berries may take longer. Remove from the heat and cool. It will thicken more as it cools.

Now if the strawberries have put you in the mood for love, but you find yourself tongue-tied, this sample "conversation" may help get you started.

An Amorous Dialogue between Thomas and Sarah; Or, The ready way of Wooing.

Thomas.

Oh my Love, how happy am I, thus accidently to meet you! Alas my dear why blush you? Why turn you that face away, on which with delight I could gaze (wou'd the brittle thread of Life continue) Ages without number.

Sarah.

Ah! How you flatter me now? Truly Tom, I did not think you had been so deep read in the Mistery of Courtship; yet I am too wise to credit all that Men say: Yes, yes, my Mother told me indeed, that men had deluding Tongues, and charged me never to trust 'em.

Thomas.

Cruel Maid, can you, after all the expressions of a real passion, which I have many ways demonstrated, believe that I am in jest or can be false?

Sarah.

Nay Tom, I know not but you may for adad, my mother says, there's not one in forty mile that mean (indeed and good earnest) what they pretend.

(The Art of courtship; or the school of delight, 1686)[74]

⌘ Fruits & Flowers ⌘

In regions like Cornwall, Devon and Kent a lot of fruit was consumed. Since many Newfoundlanders originally came from these areas, they must have craved fruits in their new home. A typical Devonshire yeoman often ate a supper of "milk and raisins boiled in a skillet served as a first course and followed by apples roasted in mead." In the seventeenth century, fruits flavoured custards, cakes and sometimes meat dishes.

Apples fried

> Pare your apples, and cut them into round slices as farre as the core; make some butter browne, and fry them with a little salt, beaten cinnamon, beaten ginger, and very little if any pepper at all; if you have some creame you may put some in, and serve after they have boyled one or two walmes.[75]

It may seem odd to eat fruit with salt and pepper, but there are some who say that these spices bring out the true flavour.

▼ ▼ ▼

1 lb. of apples cored and pared
1-2 tbsp. of butter
¼ tsp. of cinnamon
¼ tsp. of ginger
salt to taste
1 tbsp. of sugar or to taste

Core and pare the apples, then slice them. Melt butter on low heat in a frying pan and put in your seasonings. Place the apple rings in the pan, and fry on medium heat until browned. Do not leave them in too long or they will turn to mush. Sprinkle with 1 tbsp. of sugar. They may be eaten with cream, if you are not *really* worried about your cholesterol level at this point.

The ladies of Stuart times made much greater use of flowers in cookery than we do today. It made eating a colourful event. They candied violets, primroses and borage and filled tarts with flowers, spices and sugar. Marigolds dyed cheese and butter a brilliant yellow, and these golden heads also added a nice peppery flavour to meat stews. The Stuarts distilled roses into rosewater, a popular ingredient in many of their dishes. Other edible flowers included lavender, bergamot, chicory, chives, clove pinks (gillyflowers), hollyhock, hyssop, day lilies, nasturtiums, pansies, rosemary, sage, thyme flowers and, of course, the ever present dandelion.

To make conserve of flowers

To make conserve of Flowers, as Roses, Violets, Gillyflowers, and such like; you shall take the Flowers from the Stalks, and with a pair of Shears cut away the white ends at the roots thereof, and then

❧ Fruits & Flowers ☙

put them into a Stone mortar or wooden Brake, and there crush or beat them till they be come to a soft substance: and then to every pound thereof, take a pound of fine refined Sugar well searced and beat it all together, till it come to one entire body, and then pot it up, and use it as occasion shall serve.[76]

Some pie fillings were quite odd. Rosehips and even green peas were put into pies with salt, sugar and butter, topped with pastry and iced with sugar. Here's something more suitable to "modern" tastes.

To make an excellent Tart-stuffe of Damsons, to last all the yeere

Take a pottle of Damsons and good ripe Apples pared and cut into quarters, put them into an earthen pot, cover your pot with a piece of course Paste, and bake it in an Oven with Manchet and straine it through a strainer, season it with Cinnamon, Ginger, Sugar and Rose-water and boile it thick.[77]

This fruit compote has a beautiful rich colour and delicious taste.

▼ ▼ ▼

1 ½ lbs. pitted plums or damsons
1 lb. apples peeled and cut into pieces
¾ cup of sugar
½ tsp. of cinnamon
¼ tsp. of ginger
2 tbsp. of rosewater

Combine all the ingredients, except the rosewater, and cook on stovetop. Bring to the boil and then reduce the heat to medium low, cooking until thick. Strain through a strainer to get a smooth consistency and discard any skins from the plums. Stir in rosewater and chill.

Fruits & Flowers

Damsons.

To make all manner of fruit tarts. You must boil your fruit, whether it be apple, cherry, peach, damson, pear, mulberry, or codlin, in fair water, and when they be boiled enough, put them into a bowl and bruise them with a ladle, and when they be cold, strain them; and put in red wine or claret wine, and so season it with sugar, cinnamon and ginger.

(Gervaise Markham, 1656)[78]

How to make a Goosberry Fool

Take your Goosberries and pick them, and put them into clean water, and boil them til they be all as thick that you cannot discern what it is; to the value of a quart: take six yolks of eggs smal beaten with Rose-water; and before you put in your eggs, season it well with sugar, then strain your eggs, and let them boil a little while, then take it up, put it in a broad dish, and let it stand till it be cold; thus it must be eaten.[79]

▼ ▼ ▼

1 ½ lbs. of gooseberries or other fruits, cooked and strained
3 beaten egg yolks
¾ cup of sugar or sugar to taste.
2 tbsp. of rosewater
cinnamon and ginger (optional)

Stew the gooseberries until reduced, then pass them through a fine sieve. Sweeten to taste and stir in beaten yolks. Heat gently over a low heat, stirring constantly until thickened. Add rosewater. Serve in a glass dish or custard glasses. This is also nice with a touch of cinnamon and ginger as in the recipe for Tart-stuffe of Damsons.

St. John's

On the early Portuguese maps of the island, the name Rio de San Johem, or river of St. John's was used to designate the area. The Portuguese must have come into the harbour and seen the Waterford River (at that time, many times larger than it is today). The name eventually got shortened to St. John's and applied to the harbour area. This would explain how the apostrophe in the name came about.

The Europeans fished off the coasts of Newfoundland from very early on and used St. John's as a shelter for their boats and a place to carry on trade with other visiting ships. At first, the town was just a collection of fishing huts and mud paths under the fish flakes, their spindly wooden legs holding up platforms of drying, salted cod. A rough and ready place ruled by the Fishing Admirals, it must have been chaotic at the height of the fishing season, when the population swelled with thousands of fishermen arriving from the old country to farm the rich resources of the New-found-land. The stench of urine, stale beer, and rotting fish was probably smothering – especially in the summer time.

ଔ Fruits & Flowers ଲ

St. John's harbour in the late 1700s.

Planters, merchants and traders soon came and settled on the slopes leading up from the shoreline. Up here they cleared land and built houses with small gardens and livestock pens. To get away from the shore and onto the grass must have been a relief. No more slippery fish offal with every step you'd take.

In 1675, one of the early residents in St. John's was a certain Thomas Oxford. An early document states that:

> ... he and his predecessors have been possessed of houses and stages etc. in the said Harbour of St. John's for about seventy years.[80]

Other settlers at that time were the Downings, Pxons, Joyners, Loneys and a Mrs. Furzy, a widow. These people owned property and were relatively well off. For example, in 1677 John Downing owned a plantation near Virginia Lake, property at Quidi Vidi, two dwelling houses, eleven storerooms and lodging houses for fishermen, one large garden, five boats, three stages, three train vats, five rooms or flakes, thirty-seven cattle, thirty pigs and kept a Negro house servant, a real status symbol in those days! Only women of substantial means were recorded in the 1677 census. Three widows, Mrs. Sertall, Mrs. Long and Mrs. Haman were included. They employed men and women, owned boats, fishing rooms, gardens and livestock.

○₃ Section ₈○

Baking
___○₃₈○___

The kitchen was a haven of warmth, where order and civilization took away the dirt and smell of the fishery. You can be sure that no man who had not at least tried to get rid of some of the fish odour was allowed in that part of the house, especially on baking day.

The weekly baking in the seventeenth century was usually done on a Friday, and those who could afford one used a beehive shaped, clay bread oven, built into or adjacent to the fireplace. These ovens were popular in the north of Devon, and records show that at least one "cloam" oven was shipped across the ocean to Newfoundland in the mid-seventeenth century. Alternatively, many housewives in Newfoundland at the time baked their bread and cakes in an iron baking pot which was placed by the fire on a tripod. The housewife heaped hot ashes up and around the pot to bake its contents.

Pastry was used for pies and tarts, but also sealed cooking pots, allowing the contents to stew in their own juices. Sometimes a "coffin" made of rough pastry served as a cooking vessel for fillings, either sweet or savoury. It lined an oblong dish, hence the name coffin. With its filling sealed inside, it could be removed and stored for later use. Puff pastry made more delicate fruit pies and tarts. One seventeenth century recipe comes with the instructions to roll it out so thin "that ye may blow it up from the table"!

After about 1640, sugar was used a lot more as the production of sugar-cane in the West Indies increased. Newfoundland was right on the route from the West Indies to Britain, so lots of sugar, molasses and rum came our way. Large hard loaves of sugar, weighing anywhere from three to fourteen pounds, supplied the household needs. The English were well known for their "sweet tooth," and with easier access to sugar, they made more puddings and cakes, more sweets, syrups, marmalades and jams. As sugar increased in popularity, the use of heavy spices declined. This additional sugar in their food couldn't have been very good for their teeth. In the previous century, a gentleman reported that Queen Elizabeth I's were very black from her excessive use of sugar. No wonder she never married!

> The pudding is a dish very difficult to be described, because of the several sorts there are of it; flour, milk, eggs, butter, sugar, suet, marrow, raisins, etc. etc. are the most common ingredients of a pudding. They bake them in an oven, they boil them with meat, they make them fifty several ways: Blessed be he that invented pudding, for it is a manna that hits the palates of all sorts of people: a manna, better than that of the wilderness, because the people never weary of it. Ah, what an excellent thing is an English pudding! To come in pudding-time, is as much as to say, to come in the most lucky moment in the world. Give an English man a pudding, and he shall think it a noble treat in any part of the world.
>
> (M. Misson, visitor to Britain in the 1690s)[81]

Puddings could be either sweet or savoury. Here is an example of a sweet pudding, a little different from the puddings of today. It is what we would call "dunchy"– having a heavy, doughy consistency.

To make a Raspberry Pudding

> Take a quart of Cream and boil it with whole spice a while, then put in some grated Bread, and cover it off the Fire, that it may scald a little; then put in eight Eggs well beaten and sweeten it with Sugar then put in a Pint or more of whole Raspberries, and so boil it in a Cloth, and take heed you do not boil it

ଓଃ Baking ଃ୦

too much then, serve it in with Wine, Butter, and Sugar. You may sometimes leave out the Rasberries and put in Cowslip Flowers, or Goosberries.[82]

When I was growing up, the dunchier a pudding, the better it tasted.

▼ ▼ ▼

2 cups of raspberries, gooseberries, or blueberries
4 cups of dry bread crumbs
½ cup or more of brown sugar (depending on the sweetness of the fruit)
1 cup of milk or cream
3 eggs
½ tsp. each of nutmeg and cinnamon
1/8 tsp. of mace
dash of salt

Beat eggs and milk together. Add remaining ingredients. Pour the mixture into a greased bread pan or baking dish and bake at 350°F for 40 minutes or until set. Alternatively, boil the mixture in a cloth for one hour. Sprinkle extra sugar on top or serve with a fruit or brown sugar sauce.

Puddings were cooked in pudding cloths and immersed in pot liquor to cook along with the meat and vegetables. If you don't have a pudding cloth, a clean cloth napkin will do. Just put the pudding in it and tie up the corners of the napkin tightly. The Newfoundland "boiled pudding" is still a favourite dessert.

Gooseberry plant.

Baking

Port de Grave

Early settlers in Port de Grave came from Devon and Cornwall with surnames like Andrews, Butler, Anthony, Dawe, Mugford, Coveduck (Coveyduck), Tucker, Porter and Taylor. The Dawes came from Ashburton and the Mugfords from Muckford in Devon.

To make Gingerbread

Take three stale Manchets and grate them, drie them, and sift them through a fine sieve, then adde unto them one ounce of ginger beeing beaten, and as much Cinnamon, one ounce of liquorice and aniseedes being beaten together and searced, halfe a pound of sugar, then boile all these together in a posnet, with a quart of claret wine till they come to a stiffe paste with often stirring of it; and when it is stiffe, mold it on a table and so drive it thin, and print it in your moldes: dust your moldes with Cinnamon, Ginger, and liquorice, beeing mixed together in fine powder. This is your gingerbread used at the Court, and in all gentlemens houses at festival times. It is otherwise called drie Leach.[83]

The texture of this gingerbread is quite different from what we are used to.

▼ ▼ ▼

1 cup of dry white breadcrumbs
¼ tsp. ground ginger
½ tsp. cinnamon
½ tsp. aniseed, crushed
½ tsp. ground liquorice (if available)
3-4 tbsp. sugar
dash of salt
¼ cup of half and half, water/red wine

Baking

Pewter mugs and plates

Put all the ingredients in a saucepan and heat over a medium to low heat stirring constantly until a stiff dough is formed. Roll the dough out on a wooden board dusted with ground ginger and cinnamon to about ¼ inch (5mm) in thickness. Use cookie cutters, or a cookie press and cut out the dough. They can then be put in a warm oven to dry out a bit.

Women of the Time

Can you imagine what it must have been like, to be dressed in heavy, long skirts, battling your way through the snows of a hard Newfoundland winter, or suffering the heat and flies of summer while you did your many chores?

Planter women in Newfoundland did more than just run the house and take care of children. They looked after the garden, took part in the fishery, did the brewing, baking, dairying and took care of the livestock.

↜ Baking ↝

You'd think they would be very busy, but according to Britain's West Country merchants, who were very much against settlement on the island, the settlers were letting... "their womenfolk debauch ignorant mariners."

Newfoundland women were a strong breed. Widowed females either took over the family business, or found another man to marry fairly quickly. I doubt there was much problem there, as the men outnumbered the women by quite a bit. Joan Clay of Bay Roberts started with one boat and four male servants in 1675 after her husband died, and then a few years later doubled her business. There is no sign of her on the next census, so no doubt she met a man and got married again. Mary Weymouth of Carbonear was another woman who ran her own plantation in 1680. Some of the women listed at Ferryland in 1622 were Mary Russell, Sibell Dee, Elizabeth Kerne and Jone Jackson. The married women were Elizabeth Sharpus, wife of William the Tailor, Anne Bayly,

James I

wife of John, and a Widdow Bayly. Two well-known ladies of the time were Sarah Kirke, wife of the governor Sir David Kirke, and Lady Francis Hopkins. The Hopkins arrived in Ferryland in 1645. It is thought that her husband, Sir Ralph Hopkins, was killed during the English civil war. Both the Hopkins and the Kirkes were staunch Royalists. There is some evidence to suggest that Lady Hopkins was either David Kirke's sister, or sister-in-law. Lady Kirke successfully ran a large fishing business on her own after her husband was ordered back to England. Lady Francis Hopkins also ran the family plantation in Ferryland.

These ladies probably enjoyed minced meat pies at special times during the year. The earliest recipe they would have used would have contained meat. When it was discovered that the fruit mixture kept much longer on its own, they no longer added the meat. Here is an old version that contains a leg of mutton

Minced Meat

> Take a legge of Mutton, and cut the best of the flesh from the bone, and parboyl it well; then put to it three pound of the best Mutton-suet, and shred it very small; then spread it abroad and season it with Salt, Cloves and mace: then put in good store of Currants, great Raisins and Prunes clean washed and picked, a few Dates sliced and some Orange-pills sliced; then being all well mix'd together, put it into a Coffin, or into divers Coffins, and so bake them: and when they are served up, open the lids, and strew store of Sugar on the top of the meat, And in this sort you may also bake Beef or Veal, only the Beef would not be parboyl'd and the Veal will ask a double quantity of Suet.[84]

A "White pot" was an early form of bread and butter pudding.

With many Newfoundlanders coming originally from the Devon area, this recipe came over with them.

Devonshire white pot

> Take a pint of Cream and strain four Eggs into it, and put a little salt and a little sliced Nutmeg, and season it with sugar somewhat sweet, then take almost a penny Loaf of fine bread sliced very thin, and put it into a dish that will hold it, the Cream and the Eggs being put to it, then take a handful of Raisins of the Sun being boiled, and a little sweet Butter, so bake it.[85]

○₃ Baking ○○

This is very light and delicious when eaten straight from the oven.

▼ ▼ ▼

5-6 slices of white bread, crusts removed
1 tbsp. of butter
¼ cup of raisins
2 eggs
2 cups of single cream or milk
½ cup of sugar
¼ tsp. grated nutmeg
¼ tsp. salt

Line the baking dish with the sliced bread. Mix the raisins and the butter with beaten eggs and cream. Stir in the nutmeg, salt and sugar. Pour over the bread and allow it to stand for 10 minutes. Bake at 350°F for 40-50 minutes.

If you are watching your weight, you might like to keep this in mind:

Wherefore the surest way in feeding is to leave with an appetite according to the olde saying, and to keepe a corner for a friende.[86]

Blancmange evolved from a meat dish made with shredded capon (chicken), meat or fish. It gradually became a meatless dessert made with cream, sugar and rosewater, and thickened with egg yolks or beaten egg whites. A favourite Newfoundland dessert even up until the early part of the twentieth century, this sweet blancmange was also called "white leach."

Baking

The dairy

To make leach of Almonds [Blancmange]

Take halfe a pound of sweet Almonds and beat them in a mortar; then straine them with a pinte of sweet milke from the cow; then put to it one grain of muske, 2 spoonfuls of Rose-water, two ounces of fine sugar; the weight of three whole shillings of isinglasse that is very white and so boil them, then let all run thorow a strainer, then you may slice the same, and so serve it.[87]

∽ Baking ∾

▼ ▼ ▼

½ cup of sugar

2 cups of whole milk

1 tbsp. gelatine soaked in ¼ cup of the warmed milk

¼ cup of ground almonds or 1 tsp. of almond flavouring

1 tsp. of rosewater

Scald the milk and sugar in a saucepan and take out ¼ cup. Mix the gelatine with this milk and then add it to the saucepan with the other ingredients. Bring the mixture gently to the boil stirring constantly. Pour it into a jug, and when nearly cold, transfer it into a well-oiled mold. Chill for several hours and then turn out carefully on a dish. Serve on its own or with jelly.

> Our English Housewife must be of chaste thoughts, stout courage, patient, untired, watchful, diligent, witty, pleasant, constant in friendship, full of good Neighbour-hood, wise in discourse, but not frequent therein, sharp and quick of speech, but not bitter or talkative, secret in her affairs, comfortable in her Counsels, and generally skilful in all the worthy knowledges which do belong to her vocation.
>
> (Gervaise Markham, 1656)[88]

Unfortunately, I couldn't find a description of the favourable attributes to be found in a man of that time. I'm sure it couldn't have been more demanding than what they asked for in a housewife.

⊰ Baking ⊱

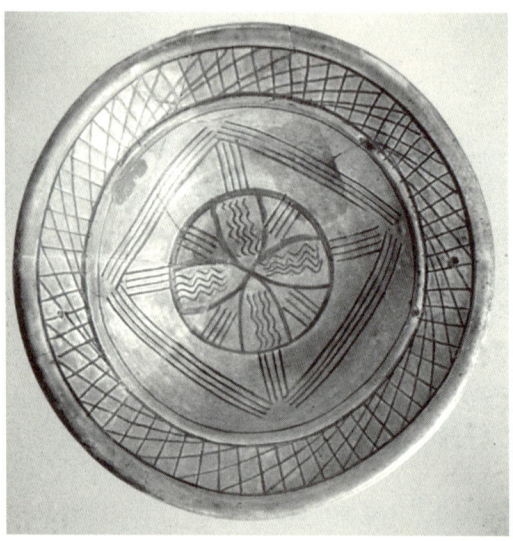

A sgraffito bowl. Fine pottery was a status symbol.
(Courtesy of MUN Archaeology Unit.)

To make Misers for Children to eat in Afternoons in Summer

Take half a pint of good small Beer, two spoonfuls of Sack, the Crum of half a penny Manchet, two handfuls of Currans washed clean and dried, and a little Nutmeg, and a little Sugar, so give it to them cold.[89]

I bet that kept them quiet!

Teenagers were a problem even then.

Life in the colonies was a sobering experience for nineteen-year-old Thomas Willoughby. He got in trouble at home in England, and was promptly shipped off to the "colonies" to gain some maturity. Here on the island, he quickly learned how rough life could get.

Among other trials, he was "thrown into an icy stream for neglecting to turn the drying fish. Writing home, he expressed suitable penitent sentiments and resolutions to 'leave aside idel vices which is not for my good,' and become 'a newe man'" (Cell, 1969, taken from a letter written in 1612, Middleton ms.)[90]

Captain Wynne of Ferryland wrote a letter to England and made a request for various tradesmen and labourers. He was adamant that "no more boyes and girles be sent hither, I meane upon your Honours charge, not any other persons which have [not] been brought up to labour: for they are unfit for these affaires."

To make Hasty Pudding

> Take one quart of Cream and boil it, then put in two Manchets Grated, and one pound almost of currans plumped, a little Salt, Nutmeg and Sugar, and a little Rosewater, and so let them boil together, stirring them continually over the fire, till you see the butter arise from the Cream, and then pour it into a Dish and serve it in with fine Sugar strewed on the brims of the Dish.[91]

This was, of course, a pudding made "in haste." It was popular in southern and midland Britain. A thick bread and milk pottage, it was prepared by boiling milk or cream and breadcrumbs together with butter, raisins, currants, spices, flour and sugar. These rich puddings certainly must have kept out the cold and damp and supplied the energy needed to keep up with a demanding life.

▼ ▼ ▼

2 cups of milk
¼ cup of brown sugar
2 cups of dry bread crumbs

1 cup of raisins
⅛ tsp. of nutmeg.
1 tbsp. of rose-water
a pinch of salt

Bring the milk to a boil and add the spice, rosewater, sugar, salt and raisins. Pour in the bread crumbs and stir continuously until a thick "pudding" is formed. Serve with wine or cream.

Bay Bulls

Bay Bulls is a picturesque little community not far from St. John's. It lies on the Southern Shore just up from Ferryland.

By 1665, a handful of families lived in Bay Bulls. Thomas Cruse, a resident in the settlement, operated a "tippling house" or tavern, so there must have been enough people to support his business, or perhaps the tourist trade was good.

A Pippin pie

Take of the fairest and best Pippins, and pare them, and make a hole in the top of them: then prick in each hole a Clove or two, then put them into the Coffin, then break in whole sticks of Cinnamon, and slices of Orange pills and Dates, on the top of every Pippin a little piece of sweet Butter: then fill the coffin, and cover the Pippins over with Sugar: then close up the Pye and bake it, as you bake Pyes of the like nature, and when it is bak'd anoint the lid over with store of sweet Butter, and then strew Sugar upon it a good thickness, and set it into the oven again for a little space, as whilst the meat is in dishing up, and then serve it.[92]

✥ Baking ✥

Apple pies were a favourite in Stuart times. They were baked with candied orange peels, cloves, cinnamon and dates to give them extra flavour, and rosewater was often added.

▼ ▼ ▼

4 large apples
1 tsp. of cinnamon
pinch of cloves
1 tbsp. of grated orange rind
¼ cup of chopped dates
¼ cup of brown sugar
2 tbsp. of butter
Add a pinch of ground cloves to each apple.

Core the apples and put them in a baking dish. Combine the cinnamon, grated orange peel, chopped dates and brown sugar and place in each apple, dividing the amounts evenly between them. Cover and bake in a moderate oven at 375°F for 20-30 minutes. This may be covered with a crust if desired, but it's not necessary.

ଓଃ Section ଃଠ

Bread Making

A friend of mine who grew up in a small rural community in Newfoundland described his mother's frustration after having worked all morning making bread for the week. By lunch time, she watched it disappear as nine hungry children stuffed themselves with almost all of the delicious, freshly baked loaves. Bread, for centuries, has been the mainstay of the Newfoundland diet. If you were hungry as a child, you ate bread with butter and molasses. We had bread with all our meals and toasted it for breakfast, spread with sugar and cinnamon or butter and jam.

In the seventeenth century the bakers made several types of bread. The very best was manchet, or white bread, often enriched with butter, eggs or milk. A coarser bread made with whole wheat flour was called Cheat bread. "Ravelled cheat" was even more branny. Brown bread was the most branny, and for poorer households, bread was made out of rye, oat, barley, pea or bean flour. The latter was not very palatable.

The upper classes favoured fine white bread. Since the Middle Ages, pale-coloured foods were held in high esteem. White bread was also much easier to digest.

When making bread, the baker mixed the flour and ale barm with a dough paddle and then kneaded it in a bread machine called a brake, or else it was "wrapped in cloth and troden upon for a good space together." They crossed it to let the devil out, a tradition still carried out in some Newfoundland households. You take your finger and push it into the dough four times to make the points of a cross. Only then can you be sure that the bread will rise. Left for an hour to "prove," the bread was shaped into round loaves and baked.

ೞ Bread Making ಬಲ

The base of a cloam oven found at Ferryland. Inset: detail of oven.
(Courtesy of MUN Archaeology Unit.)

The receypte of the Dyett bread

> Take halfe a pecke of Fyne Wheaten Flower, three handfull of sage shredd small, An ounce and a halfe of ordinary Fennell seede lightly bruised, strawe the sage and the Fennell seede amongst the Flower, and so with barme kneade and bake ytt as you do other breade, and eate ytt nott until ytt be a day old. [93]

This is at its best straight out of the oven, spread with butter and served with a soup.

▼ ▼ ▼

4 cups of plain flour

1 tsp. sage (powdered) or three tbsp. of fresh (chopped)

1 tsp. crushed fennel seed

2 cups of warm water or enough to make a soft dough

1 package of dried yeast mixed with 1 tsp. sugar and ½ cup of the warm water. Follow the directions on the package.

½ tsp. of salt (optional)

Mix the dry ingredients in a warm bowl and work in the yeast mixture and the remaining 1 ½ cups of liquid. Knead and leave to rise in a warm place for 1 hour. Knead again on a floured board, shape into two round loaves and let it rise for a further 30 minutes before baking at 350°F for 30-40 minutes.

And if you're tempted to have just one more slice, remember these wise words:

> Use a measure in eating that thou mayst live long and if thou wilt be in health, then hold thine handes.[94]

Of baking manchets

Now for the baking of Bread of your simple meals, your best and principal bread is Manchet, which you shall bake in this manner; first your Meal, being ground upon the black stones if it be possible, which makes the whitest flour, and bolted through the finest bolting cloth, you shall put it into a clean Kimnel, and opening the flour hollow in the midst, put into it of the best Ale Barm the quantity of three pints to a bushel of meal, with some Salt to season it with: then put in your Liquor reasonable warm and knead it very well together both with your hands and through the brake; or for want thereof, fold it in a cloth, and with your feet tread it a good space together, then, letting it lie an hour or thereabouts to swett, take it forth and mould it into Manchets, round, and flat; scotch about the waist to give it leave to rise, and prick it with your knife in the top, and so put it into the Oven, and bake it with a gentle heat.[95]

Never take up food with hands not washed.
Let no one take food until the blessing be given, nor take a seat, except that which the master of the house chooses.
While you are sitting at the table, think first of the poor man,
For when you are full of meat, you know not what the needy man feels.

Avoid eating of the dishes until they are put before you.

Cut the bread which he bids you cut who wants some of it.

("How to bear yourself at table")[96]

To make Spiced bread

Take two pound of Manchet paste, sweet Butter half a pound, Currans half a pound, Sugar a quarter, and a little Mace (if you wil put in any) and make it into a loafe, and bake it in an Oven no hotter then for Manchet.[97]

Spice bread was very popular with the gentry as a breakfast food in the late-seventeenth century. This looks very similar to Newfoundland raisin bread, a staple in outport households.

▼ ▼ ▼

4 cups of plain flour

½-1 tsp. mace

1 ½ cups of warm water or enough to make a soft dough

1 package of dried yeast mixed with 1 tsp. sugar and ½ cup of the warm water. Follow the directions on the package.

½ tsp. of salt (optional)

¼ cup of butter or lard, melted

1 egg

1 cup of raisins or currants

Mix the dry ingredients in a warm bowl and work in the yeast mixture with the butter and egg and the remaining liquid. Knead and leave to rise in a warm place for 1 hour. Knead again on a floured board, shape into two round loaves and let it rise for a further 30 minutes before baking at 350°F for 30-40 minutes.

Bread Making

To make bisket bread, otherwise called French bisket

Take a half a peck of fine flower, two ounces of coriander seeds, one ounce of annis seedes and the whites of four eggs. A half pint of ale yeast and as much water as will make it up into stiff paste. Your water must be but blood warme, then bake it in a long roll as big as your thigh. Let it stay in the oven but one hour. When it is a day old pare it and slice it , then sugar it over with fine powdered sugar and so dry it in an oven again, and being dry, take it out and sugar it again, then box it and so you may keep it all the year.[98]

Do you catch yourself wondering how large their thighs were? This recipe produced a lot of biscuit dough! (A peck equals about 32 cups of flour). For more reasonable portions try this:

▼ ▼ ▼

3 cups of flour
1 tbsp. coriander seed (crushed)
1 tbsp. anise seed (crushed)
½ cup of sugar
1 egg white
1 package of yeast.
1 tsp. of sugar
enough warm water to make a soft dough

Dissolve yeast as per instructions on the package, using ½ cup of the warm water. Gradually mix in sifted flour, spice mixture (I grind my spices in a coffee grinder kept specifically for that purpose), sugar and egg white. Add enough water to make a soft dough, about one cup. Let it rise one hour. Punch it down and form into a roll (perhaps as big around as your arm!). Let rise again, place on a baking sheet and bake for about 20-30 minutes at 350°F. Let it cool completely and then slice it thinly and sprinkle sugar over it. Toast it lightly in a

Placentia – The great beach. (Courtesy of Amanda Crompton.)

warm oven. The sugar will melt and form a sort of icing. Remove from oven and sprinkle with sugar again. Store in a sealed container.

Placentia

Placentia stretches across a bar of flat land, reaching out into the bay. The surrounding mountains sit like watchful parents guarding the town. The spot was well chosen, because it was easy to defend. The fortress on top of Castle Hill had cannon for just that purpose.

In 1658 Louis XIV granted Nicolas Gargot de la Rochette land on the west side of the Avalon Peninsula. The grant included Placentia and the governorship of the new colony. Eighty settlers and thirty soldiers established a settlement there in 1662, and the population increased steadily until the mid-1690s. Many of the new settlers were fishermen from the Basque region of France.

◊ Bread Making ◊

It wasn't long before Placentia became a thriving community. In addition to the dwelling houses there was a governor's house, a church, monastery and several buildings of commerce. The French king encouraged colonization, and gave a free food allowance to the new settlers for their first year. He encouraged families with marriageable daughters to emigrate to Placentia, and the food allowance for them was increased to three years. The French also welcomed English settlers.

The governor and a few other residents formed a sort of "upper class" in the colony, wining, dining, hunting in the surrounding woods and indulging in other pleasures. In 1685, Governor Parat became embroiled in a scandal, living openly with the wife of one of the citizens of Placentia. The chaplain, Père Cordelier Laurent Morin, also had a mistress. The residents of course complained and Parat was given a warning by the king to give up his mistress. He did so, but soon after imported another one, a Mme. Delisle, from Paris. This lady bore him several children, and the scandal gradually died down. It seems nothing much was said to the priest!

Saintonge bowl found at Placentia.
(Courtesy of Amanda Crompton).

◯ Bread Making ◯

After all that rich food, it's time to settle back and enjoy a drink or two, some good conversation, and a few pipe-fulls of tobacco.

Smoking was a popular pastime. (Courtesy of Steve Mills.)

Section

Drink

People drank many different things in the seventeenth century, but water wasn't one of them. It was considered "not holesome sole by it selfe, for an Englyshe man." Edward Garton of Cupids supposedlly died because of hard work and "much drinking of water in the winter." (Robert Rossell and William Hatton, 1613)[99]

So what did they drink?

(Courtesy of Colony of Avalon Foundation)

Ale for an Englyshe man is a natural drynke.

(Andrew Boorde, 1542)[100]

Almost everyone drank beer, small ale or ale with their meals, even the children. Ale was aged and higher in alcohol content than "small ale," a weaker drink which the housewife brewed weekly or bi-weekly. Beer was ale flavoured with hops. These hops acted as a preservative and guarded the brew from contaminating bacteria often left in the barrels. Some brews had herbs and spices added, others the

A drinking scene.

juices of flowers and fruits. There must have been some very interesting drinking going on.

> But if you will make a right Gossips cup, that shall farre exceed all the Ale that ever mother Bunch made in her life time, then in bottling up of your best Ale, tun halfe a pint of white Ipocrasse that is newly made, and after the best receipt, with a pottle of Ale: stop your bottle close, and drinke it when it is Stale. Some commend the hanging of roasted Orenges prickt full of Cloves in the vessell of Ale, till you find the taste thereof sufficiently graced to your owne liking.
>
> (Sir Hugh Platt, 1611)[101]

⊗ Drink ⊗

David Kirke came from a family of wine merchants and imported a lot of wine into the colonies. He became governor of the Colony of Avalon in 1638. Kirke and other merchants exported Newfoundland fish to the southern European countries. They traded fish for wine and other luxury goods from the Mediterranean markets. Archaeologists have discovered pieces of expensive wine glasses and the bottle fragments of imported beverages at sites here on the island.

Aqua vitae was a drink produced from distilled wine or ale. This was a proof spirit with four parts alcohol to one part water with some aniseeds and sugar syrup put in for flavouring. In one letter sent from Newfoundland to England, a request was made not to send out meal and malt for the making of beer, but to just send more Aqua Vitae. When the Irish came later in the century, they translated the Latin name, into Gaelic. It became "uisge Beatha" which in turn got corrupted into whiskey.

Rum made an appearance by the middle of the century and is still a very popular drink here. Made in the West Indies, the merchants in Newfoundland imported it in large quantities.

One individual in Barbados observed:

> The chief fuddling they make in the island [Barbados] is rumbullion, alias killdevil, and this is made of sugar cones distilled, a hot hellish and terrible liqour.[102]

Well, we liked it! A version of this is still available today. It is called "Screech."

With the amount of alcohol consumed here, no doubt the "Newfoundland housewife" was kept busy calling her husband "home from his error."

> It is meet that our English Housewife be a woman of great modesty and temperance as well inwardly as

outwardly: Inwardly, as in her behaviour and carriage towards her Husband wherein she shall shun all violence of rage, passion, and humour, coveting less to direct than to be directed, appearing ever unto him pleasant, amiable, and delightful; And, tho' occasion of mishaps, or the mis-government of his will may induce her to contrary thoughts, yet virtously to suppress them, and with a mild sufferance rather to call him home from his error, than with the strength of anger to abate the least spark of his evil, calling into her mind that evil and uncomely language is deformed though uttered even to Servants, but most monstrous and ugly when it appears before the presence of a Husband.

(Gervase Markham, 1656)[103]

Spruce Beer

Spruce beer was originally brewed by the native people. The early settlers learned it from the natives and then "improved it." Used

Spigot found at Placentia. (Courtesy of Amanda Crompton.)

as a cure for scurvy, it worked well, possibly due to the vitamin C content in the spruce boughs. This brew could also be mixed with rum to make a drink called callibogus. That concoction was probably strong enough to cure anything.

> Take a copper that Contains 12 Gallons fill it as full of the Boughs of Black spruce as it will hold Pressing them down pretty tight fill it up with water Boil it till the Rind will strip off the Spruce Boughs which will waste it bout one third take them out & add to the water one Gallon of Melasses Let the whole Boil till the Melasses are disolvd take a half hogshead & Put in nineteen Gallons of water & fill it up with the Essence. Work it with Barm or Beer grounds & in Less than a week it is fit to Drink.
>
> (Joseph Banks, 1766)[104]

To make Hippocras

> To make Ippocras, take a pottle of Wine, two Ounces of good Cinnamon, half an ounce of Ginger, nine Cloves, and six Pepper corns, and a Nutmeg, and bruise them and put them into the wine with some Rosemary flowers, and so let them steep all night, and then put in Sugar a pound at least; and when it is well settled, let it run through a wollen bag made for that purpose: thus if your Wine be Claret, the Ippocras will be red; if white, then of that colour also.[105]

▼ ▼ ▼

1 bottle of red wine
¼ cup of sugar or to taste
4 sticks of cinnamon, broken up
3 thin slices of fresh ginger
5 whole cloves

dash of nutmeg
3 peppercorns
1 tsp. rosemary flowers (optional)

Combine ingredients and put in a closed container to steep overnight. The next evening you may remove the whole spices and serve.

Torbay

One of the nicest trails to walk in the St. John's area is the East Coast Trail that runs along the cliffs of Torbay. These cliffs form the walls of the bay and are full of deep crevices and caves. Rumors of pirate gold abound.

Between 1620 and 1623 a pirate named John Nutt did frequent the area. A scoundrel, but a trusting one, Nutt negotiated a pardon with Sir John Eliot, Vice-Admiral of Devon. He was told to return to England with the sum of £500 and then collect his pardon. When he arrived, Eliot had him thrown in jail and sentenced to hang. Nutt had good friends in high places, though, and George Calvert (Lord Baltimore of Ferryland fame) had Nutt released and Eliot imprisoned and fined 100 pounds, payable to Nutt. There is justice after all.

Torbay's first citizen was a man by the name of Dennis McCarthy. He spent what was probably a very miserable winter living in a fisherman's shed. Another fisherman joined him and the two settled there and became coopers. They probably made a good living servicing the fishing vessels which stored their catch in barrels. When the census was taken in 1677, their descendants were still living in Torbay.

The true bottling of Beere

> When your Beere is ten or twelve dayes old, whereby it is growne reasonable cleere, then bottle it, making your corkes very fit for the bottles, and stop them close: but drink not of this beere, till they begin to work again and mantle, and then you shall find the

same most excellent and spritely drink: and this is the reason why bottle-ale is both so windy and muddy, thundering and smoking upon the opening of the bottle, because it is commonly bottled the same day that it is laid into the cellar; whereby its yeast, being an exceeding windy substance, being also drawn

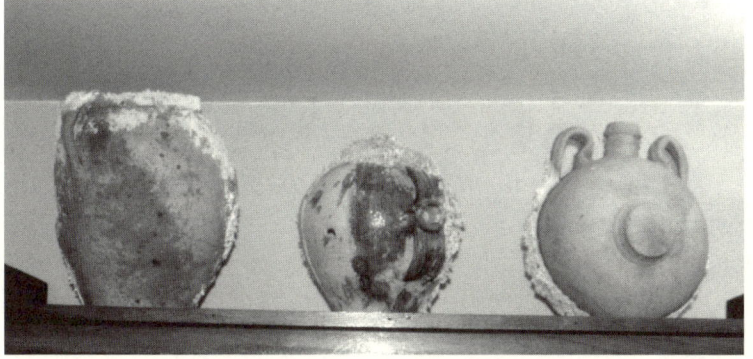

Storage pots. (Courtesy of MUN Archaeology Unit.)

with the ale not yet fine, doth incorporate with the drink, and maketh it also very windy: and this is all the Lime and Gun-powder wherewith bottle-ale hath beene along time so wrongfully charged.[106]

The English Merchants, intent on being spoil sports, put a ban on the sale of liquor in "tippling houses" in Newfoundland.

That noe person doe set up any Taverne for sellinge of wyne, Beere, or stronge waters, cyder or Tobacco, to entertayne the fishermen, because it is found that by such meanes they are debauched, neglecting thar labors and poore ill governed men not only spend most part of their shares before they come home, upon which the life and mayntenance of their wife and Children depende but are likewise hurtfull in divers other waies, as by labour, by purloyninge and stealinge...

(Star Chamber Rules, 1633)[107]

I'm sure they wouldn't have objected to alcohol used for medicinal purposes.

William Vaughan, the Welsh poet and adventurer who sent settlers out to his colony in the Renews area, had a remedy for seasickness. It was "Worme-wood wine or salt of worme-wood in Beere or wine."

Wormwood was a main ingredient in the famous drink known as absinth or Green Fairy, very popular in Paris at the turn of the last century.

Wormwood wine

> Take a handful of dried Wormwood for every gallon of wine, stop it in a vessel close, and so let it remain in steep. So is prepared Wine of Rosemary-flowers and Eye-bright.[108]

To make a syllabub

> My Lady Middlesex makes Syllabubs for little Glasses with spouts, thus Take 3 pints of sweet Cream, one of quick white wine (or Rhenish), and a good wine glassful (better the ¼ of a pint) of Sack :mingle them with about three quarters of a pound of fine Sugar in Powder. Beat all these together with a whisk, till all appeareth converted into froth. Then pour it into your little Syllabub-glasses, and let

them stand all night. The next day the Curd will be thick and firm above, and the drink clear under it. I conceive it may do well to put into each glass (when you pour your liquor into it) a sprig of Rosemary a little bruised, or a little Lemon-peel, or some such thing to quicken the taste...or Nutmegs, or Mace, or Cloves, a very little.[109]

This recipe is really worth trying. Once you have one glass of this you won't want to stop!

▼ ▼ ▼

2 cups of whipping cream
¾ cup of red or white wine (red gives it a nice warm colour)
⅓ cup dry sherry
½ cup of sugar
sprigs of rosemary or ground nutmeg

Beat all the ingredients except the rosemary together and then pour the mixture into any fine glassware. Put a sprig of rosemary into each glass or sprinkle with nutmeg and refrigerate for a day or overnight. The liquid will separate and this is as it should be. In 1655, another set of directions for making syllabub stated that the cream must be spooned in "… as hard as you can, as though you milk it in."

Drink

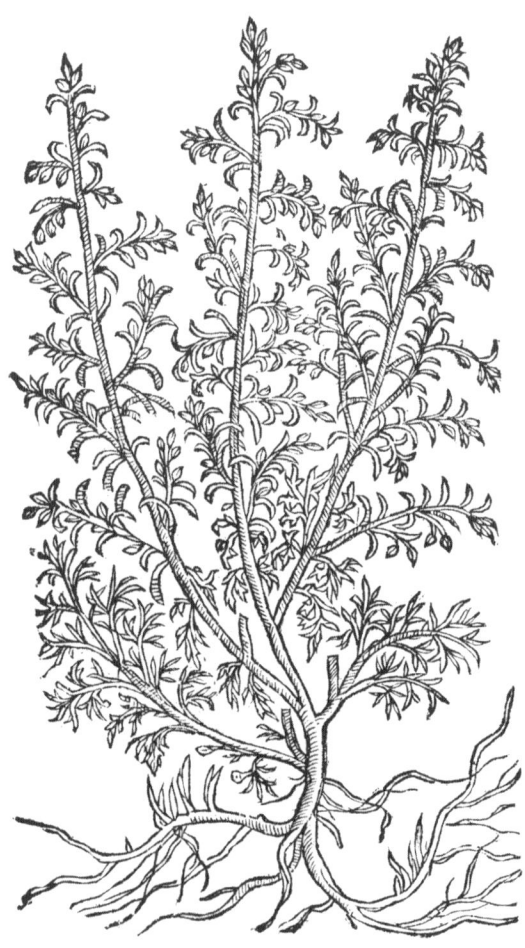

Sea Wormewood.

Section

Miscellanea

In those days, the way to preserve milk was to turn it into butter or cheese. In West Country England, Bristol and in the ports of Somerset, Welsh cheese was well liked and described as being "very tender and Palatable." No doubt some of this made its way to Newfoundland, and they may possibly have even tasted cheddar cheese, which was first made in England in the seventeenth century. Now if you didn't have a cow or your cow didn't survive the Newfoundland winter, ewe's or goat's milk could also be made into strong cheese.

Butter and mustard were favourite condiments which went with just about anything, and mustard pickles, mint sauce and apple sauce also added zest to their meals. The most common sauce was gravy, made from the thickened meat juices flavoured with verjuice or wine. Another extremely popular condiment was made with shredded horseradish, milk or cream and verjuice.

Sauces recommended by Robert May, author of *The Acomplisht Cook* (1660), were:

"strained prunes, wine and sugar" or "white wine, gravy, large mace, and butter thickened with two or three yolks of eggs."

Miscellanea

Butter was coloured with marigolds.

How to draw your butter thicke

Put to every pound of butter, sixe spoonefuls of vinegar, a branch of Rosemary, a little whole mace & a few cloves, put them into an earthen pipkin, or a pewter dish, and set them upon a few coales, and when the butter begins to melt, take a ladle and poure it up a high till it be all melted and then it will be as thick as creame and serve to butter any fresh fish.[110]

Miscellanea

▼ ▼ ▼

1 cup of butter
3 tbsp. vinegar
½ tsp. of rosemary
¼ tsp. each of mace and cloves

Melt your butter on low heat and add the vinegar and flavourings.

To make Clove or Cinnamon Sugar

Lay pieces of Sugar in close boxes amongst stickes of Cinnamon, Cloves, &c. And in short time it will purchase both the taste and sent of the spice.[111]

And for the "Martha Stewarts" of the seventeenth century:

How to hang your candles in the ayre without candlestickes

This will make a strange shew to the beholders that know not the conceit. It is done in this manner: let a fine Virginall wyar be conveyed in the midst of every weeke, and left of some length above the candle, to fasten the same to the posts in the roofe of your house: and if the roome be anything high roofed, it will bee hardly discerned, and the flame, thaough it consume the tallow yet it will not melt the wyar.[112]

Somehow I have visions of flaming candles dripping or dropping on the heads of dinner guests.

Miscellanea

❦ Section ❧

Cures
❦❧

In 1602, William Vaughan published his *Fifteen Directions to preserve Health*. Life in the seventeenth century seemed to be dominated by rules for everything. I suppose it gave them a sense of security in a dangerous world where so much was left to chance. In Newfoundland the dangers and challenges of adapting to a new and strange environment must have encouraged them to take very good care of themselves.

> First of all in the morning when you are about to rise, stretch your self strongly: for thereby the animall heate is somewhat forced into the outward partes, the memorie is quickned, and the bodie strengthened.
> Secondarily, rub and chafe your body with the palmes of your hands, or with a course linnen cloth; the breast, back and belly, gently; but the armes, thighes, and legges roughly, till they seem ruddy and warme
> Evacuate your selfe.
> Put on your apparell.
> When you have apparelled your selfe hansomely, combe your head softly and easily with an Ivorie combe: for nothing recreateth the memorie more.
> Picke and rub your teeth: and because I would not have you to bestow much cost in making dentrifices for them; I will advertise you by foure rules of importance how to keepe your teeth white and uncorrupt, and also to have a sweete breath. First, wash well your mouth when you have eaten your meat: sec-

ondly, sleepe with your mouth somewhat open. Thirdly, spit out in the morning that which is gathered together that night in the throate: then take a linnen cloth, and rub your teeth well with and without, to take away the fumositie of the meat and the yellownesse of the teeth for it is that which putrifieth them and infecteth the breath.

Wash your face, eyes, eares and hands, with fountaine water.

When you have finished these say your morning prayers.

Goe about your businesse circumspectly, and endeavour to banish all cares and cogitations, which are the onely baits of wickednesse.

Eat three meales a day until you come to the age of fourtie yeares: as, your breakefast, dinner, and supper: yet that betweene breakefast and dinner there be the space of foure houres, and betwixt dinner and supper seaven houres: the breakfast must be lesse then dinner, and the dinner somewhat lesse then supper.

Labour not either your mind or body presently after meales: rather sit a while and discourse of some pleasant matters: when you have ended your confabulations, wash your face and mouth with cold waters then go to your chamber, and make cleane your teeth with your tooth-picker, which should be either of ivorie, silver, or gold.

Put of your clothes in winter by the fire side: and cause your bed to bee heated with a warming panne.

Cures

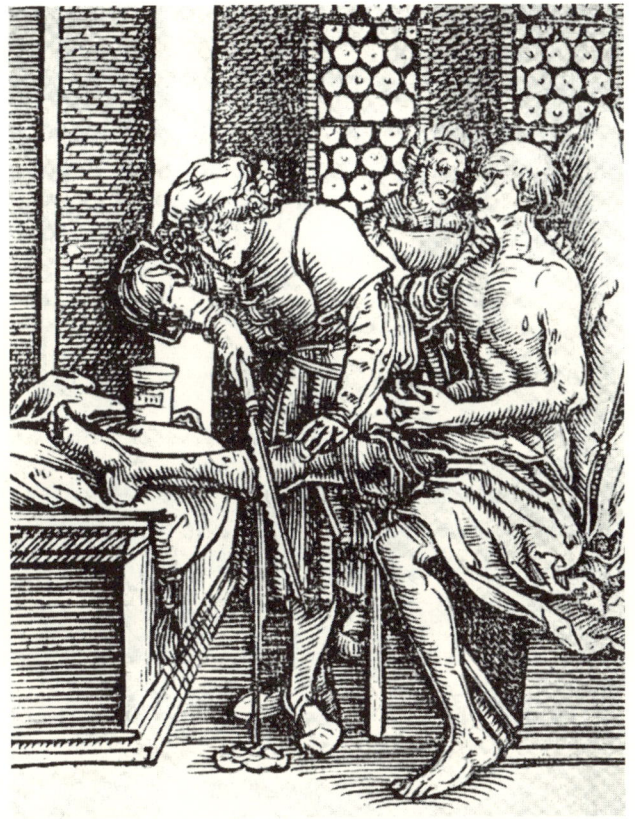

Prevention was always better than the cure.

Remember before you rest, to chew down two or three drachmes of mastick; for it will preserve your body from bad humours.
Pray fervently to God, before you sleep, to inspire you with his grace.
In the morning remember you affayres and if you be trouble with rheumes, as soone as you have risen, eate white pepper now and then, and you shall be holpen.[113]

Syrup of Turnips

> First bake the Turnips in a pot with houshold bread, then press out the liqour between two platter: put a pint of this liqour to half a pint of Hysop water and as much brown sugar candy as will sweeten it; and boil it to the consistance of a syrup.
>
> It is very good for a cold or consumption.[114]

One harsh winter in Newfoundland, the settlers discovered that eating turnips was:

> ... excedding good for scarby [scurvy]... and we at one tyme some six weekes s[ince], more than halfe of our company verie sicke and lame in [this] disease; so rasing ther Rootes eatting them raw in very short ty[me] yet did help them all so they are excellent for that propose and will serve for meat allso: they do eatt verie dilligate
>
> (Henry Crout in a letter from Cupids, 1613)[115]

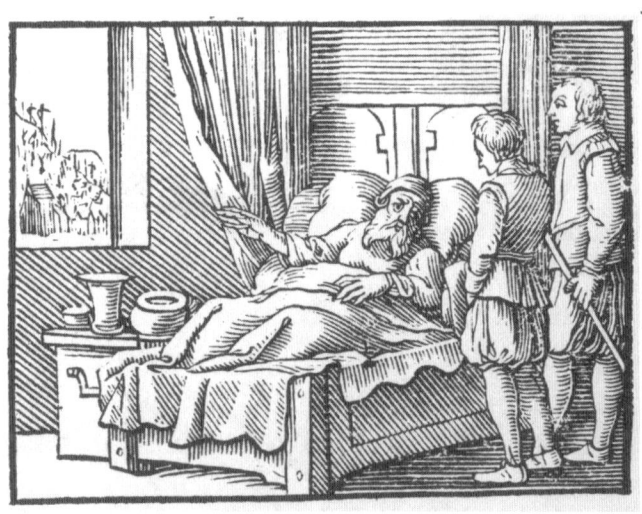

⊛ Cures ⊛

1613 saw a much rougher winter than they were used to and the Cupid's colony had twenty-two people down with scurvy. Eight of the sick died.

A Recipe to help Digestion

> Take two quarts of Small Ale, put to it red mints one handful, as much of red sage, a little cinnamon, let it boil softly till half be wasted; sweeten it with sugar to your taste and drink thereof a draught morning and evening.[116]

For a Sore Throat

> Mingle burnt Allum, the yolk of an Egg, powder of white Dogs turd, and some honey together; tye a clout on the end of a stick wet in this mixture and therewith rub the throat; or mix white Dogs turd with honey spread it on sheeps leather and apply it to the throat.[117]

Women throughout history have ministered to the sick. Although Mr. Markham seems to think some medical knowledge is useful in a woman, he is somewhat less than enlightened in other ways. He would be treading on dangerous ground if he uttered these thoughts today.

> One of the most principal vertues which doth belong to our English Housewife; you shall understand, that with the preservation and care of the family touching their health and soundness of body consisteth most in the diligence of her, it is meet that she have a Physical kind of knowledge; how to

administer many wholesom receipts or medicines for the good of their healths, as well to prevent the first occasion of sickness, as to take away the effects and evil of the same, when it hath made seisure on the body.

Indeed we must confess, that the depth and secrets of this most excellent Art of Physic are far beyond the capacity of the most skilful woman, as lodging only in the brest of the learned Professors, yet that our Housewife may from them receive some ordinary rules and medicines, which may avail for the benefit of her family, is (in our common experience) no derogation at all to that worthy Art.

(Gervase Markham, 1656)[118]

The lady Drury's Medicine for the cholick. Proved

Take a turf of green Grass, and lay it to the Navil, and let it lie till you find ease, the green side must be laid next to the belly.[119]

A Cordiall for wind in the stomack or any Part

Take six or eight spoonfuls of Pennyroyal-water, put into it four drops of oil of Cinnamon, so drink it anytime of the day, so you fast two houres after.[120]

Early English courtesy books are very definite in their condemnation of digestive wind. It was not tolerated in polite society, although there were some that had great sympathy for the afflicted.

Great harms have grown and maladies exceeding
By keeping in a little blast of wind
So cramps & dropsies, colics have their breeding
And mazed brains, for want of vent behind.
                    (Sir John Harrington, 1608)[121]

To make the Face fair and for a stinking breath

Take the flowers of rosemary and seethe them in white wine, with which wash your face; if you drink thereof, it will make you have a sweet breath.[122]

For Heat in the Face, redness and shining of the nose

Take a fair linnen cloth and in the morning lay it over the grass, and draw it over till it be wet with dew, then wring it out into a fair dish, and wet the face therwith as often as you please: as you wet it let it dry in. May dew is the best.[123]

Precious stones were considered to be an aid to health:

... alwaies in your hands use eyther Corall or yellow Amber, or a Chalcedonium, or a sweet Pommander, or some like precious stone to be worne in a ring upon

the little finger of the left hand: have in your rings eyther a smaragd, a Saphire, or a Craconites, which you shall beare for an ornament: for in stones, as also in hearbes, there is great efficacie and vertue.

(Sir John Harington, 1624)[124]

For a Cough

Take Sallade oil, Aqua vitae, and Sack, of each an equal quantity, beat them altogether, and before the fire rub the soles of your feet with it.[125]

In Winter time, warme well your garments at the fire, and warm the linings of the same, for it helpeth concoction, and removeth all humidity and moysture. But my father did not allow of this custome, warning men of strength, and those that are borne for the Common-wealth, not to accustom themselves to such kind of softness, which doe weaken our bodies.

(Sir John Harington, 1624)[126]

To stanch the bleeding of a Wound.

Take a Hounds turd, and lay it on a hot coal, and bind it thereto and that shall stanch bleeding, or else bruise a long Worm, and make pouder of it, and cast it on the wound, or take the ear of a Hare, and make pouder thereof, and cast that on the wound, and that will stanch bleeding.[127]

A Bag to smell unto for Melancholy, or to cause one to sleep

Take dry Rose leafes, keep them close in a glass which will keep them sweet, then take pouder of Mints, pouder of Cloves in a gross pouder and put the same to the Rose leaves, then put all these together in a bag, and take that to bed with you, and it will cause you to sleep, and it is good to smell unto at other times.[128]

When you put off your garments to go to bed, then put away all your cogitations, & lay them aside, whether they be publike or private, for when all your members be free from all cares, you shall then sleep the quieter, concoction and the other naturall actions shall best be performed.

(Sir John Harrington, 1624)[129]

For Pin, or Web, in the eye

Take two or three Lice out of ones head, and put them alive into the eye that is grieved, and so close it up, and most assuredly the Lice will suck out the Web in the eye, and will cure it, and come forth without any hurt.[130]

Their concern for the louse was touching.

A bedpan urinal found at Ferryland.
(Courtesy of MUN Archaeology Unit.)

To make Oil of Sage

Good for the greif in any joynt, or for any ach. Take Sage and Parsly, seeth them in the oil Olive, till it be thick and green.[131]

For the Hearing

Take an Onion, take the core out of it, fill it with Pepper, slice it in the midst, being first wrapt in Paper and roasted in the embers, lay it to each ear.[132]

Of Sage flowers

It preserveth against Melancholly, doth dry and comfort the stomack, cureth an old cough, and openeth the stopping of the liver.[133]

Cures

King Edwards perfume to make your house smell like Rosemary.

Take three spoonfuls of perfect Rosemary, and as much Sugar as half a Walnut beaten in small powder; all these boiled together in a perfuming Pan upon hot Embers with a few coals is a very sweet perfume.[134]

To cure corns

Take Beans, and chew them in your mouth, and tye salt to your corn, and it will help: do this at Night.[135]

For Consumption

Take a Pint of Red Cows milk, then take the yolk of a new laid Egg poached very rare, then stir it into the milk over a soft fire, but do not let it boil, sweeten it with a little sugar Candy and drink it in the morning fasting, and when you go to bed.[136]

A Puritan housewife.

In a letter from Cupids in 1611, John Guy wrote:

> There was one... called William Stone, having at the first only a stiffness in one of his knees kept his bed ten weekes and would never stirre his body, which lasinesse brought him to his end, who died the thirteenth of April.

Not much sympathy there! Or here:

> Of the rest foure or five have bin sicke... All of them, if they had had as good will to work, as they had good stomackes to ther victuals, would long since have bin recovered. 137

Against the trembling of the heart

> Take 3 or 4 spoonefuls of Claret-wine, and halfe as much Damask rose-water, an ounce of white sugar-candy disolved and give it the sick to drinke warme.138

To take away spots and freckles from the face or hands

> The sap that issueth out of a birch tree in great abundance being opened in March or April, with a receiver of glass, set under the boring thereof to receive the same, doth performe the same most excellent and maketh the skin very clear.
>
> The sap will dissolve pearle (a secret not known onto many)139

The secret of this recipe's success was probably due to fact that a layer of skin was removed in the process of getting the sticky sap off your face! I don't think I would try this on cataracts (pearle).

The shadows are long now in a kitchen lit only by candlelight. The housewife banks the fire, gathering the coals together to keep hot till the next morning She covers the open hearth with the curfew which will protect the household from dangerous sparks that might fly out during the night. The dishes are cleaned and the table scrubbed, ready for another day. "Rabbit," she thinks to herself. "Tomorrow we will eat rabbit." With that she guts the candle on the table and takes the remaining one in hand to see her way up to the bed chamber where her husband already lies sleeping.

Writing this book has brought me through a fascinating journey of food, history and my own heritage. It seemed like a simple enough project when I first started – just collect a few recipes and put in a bit of trivia. Well, I went to work and dug deeper and deeper and became more interested as each day passed. What started out as a simple "booklet" project, became a labour of love that stretched over many months and many volumes of British and Newfoundland history, period cookbooks, letters, books of manners and much more. I have loved every minute of time spent with these seventeenth century ladies and gentlemen and hope that this book will serve to introduce you to their world.

❧ Section ☙

Both sea and land here swarme (as it were) with benefets and blessings of God for man's use and reliefe.

(Edward Wynne to Sir George Calvert, August 1621)[140]

Section

Section

⌘ Section ⌘

Glossary:

Allum – potassium aluminum sulfate.

Barm – live yeast taken from the top of fermenting beer. It was commonly used as the yeast element in breads, cakes and batters.

Bean-cods – bean pods.

Borage – Borago officinalis, a plant with hairy leaves and bright blue flowers. Flowers can be used in salads.

Broil – in these times it meant "to grill."

Cabbage-lettuce – cabbage.

Capers – the pickled flower buds of the nasturtium plant.

Chalcedonium – a type of quartz. eg. onyx, agate, tiger's eye etc.

Chibol – a type of mild onion.

Chyrurgeon – doctor

Codlin or codling – an unripe apple.

Collops – thinly sliced meats, eg. collops of bacon.

Curfew – semicircular metal hoods (from the french couvre-feu) used to cover up the fire at night.

Fishing Admiral – the first ship's captain to arrive in the harbour at the beginning of the fishing season was given complete authority over the other ships and residents.

Groats – whole grains, sometimes crushed.

Hysop – small bushy aromatic herb with blue flowers. Genus hyssopus. Said to improve weak eyesight and relieve asthma.

Isinglasse – a form of gelatin taken from a fish (sturgeon).

Kimnel – a large tub used for preparing bread, brewing, or making cheese.

Manchet – a loaf of white bread.

Pottage – a stew of vegetables and sometimes meat. A thick soup.

❦ Section ❧

Pearle – cateracts.

Pennyroyal – a type of creeping mint, mentha pulegium.

Pippin – a tart cooking apple.

Planter – an owner of a vessel, or a fishing premises, also known as a "plantation."

Pommander – a perfumed ball carried to ward off disease.

Pottle – the equivalent of two bottles of wine, i.e. two quarts.

Purslane – the herb "portalaca oleracea."

Qualms – see "Walms."

Race – a root, eg. ginger.

Sack – a fortified wine like sherry.

Scum – to take off the froth that rises to the surface.

Seam – fat.

Seeth/sod – to boil, boiled.

Skirret – a type of water parsnip, "sium sisarum."

Small beer – weak beer.

Sops/Sippets – small triangles of dried or toasted bread.

Splatted – split open.

Stoved – to dry or preserve in a stove.

Suet – the hard white fat found around the kidneys of sheep or cows.

Umbles – the organs; liver, kidney etc.

Verjuice – a juice extracted from unripe fruit, usually crushed crabapples.

Walms/qualms – to heat or boil for a short time.

Yeoman – a man holding a small estate, could serve on juries and vote for the knight of the shire.

✿ Section ✿

Acknowledgements

I would like to thank the following:

Everyone at Flanker Press for their great patience, and Ed Kavanagh for his editing skills.

Dr. Jim Tuck, Barry Gaulton, Amanda Crompton and Steve Mills of the MUN Archaeology Unit, for checking the manuscript for historical inaccuracies and for permission to use their photographs.

Dr. Paul O'Neill for reviewing the manuscript and giving helpful suggestions.

Donna Morrissey for reviewing the manuscript.

Lil Hawkins and staff of the Colony of Avalon Foundation for all their help and also for permission to use photographs.

Mr. Bill Gilbert of the Baccalieu Trail Heritage Corp. Inc. for the use of his photographs.

Dr. Peter Pope for advice and permission to use an illustration from his Ph.D. thesis.

Ned Pratt for the beautiful cover photography.

Lillian Fidler and Danielle Percy for book and cover design.

Derek L. Frampton of Pitcher Plant Investments Inc. for his kind advice on artistic layout.

Thomson Publishing Services Co., UK for permission to use the "Pease Pottage" recipe from The Compleat Cook.

The very friendly and helpful staffs of the Centre for Newfoundland Studies in the Queen Elizabeth II library and the Newfoundland Collection in the A.C. Hunter Library.

All friends and relatives who both cooked and ate seventeenth century food.

Section

Sources

1. Gillian T. Cell, <u>Newfoundland Discovered: English attempts at Colonization 1610-1630</u> (London: Hakluyt Society, 1982), 203.

2. Richard Whitbourne, <u>A discourse and Discovery of New-found-land, 1620</u>, ed. by Dr. Hans Rollman, The Newfoundland and Labrador Pages: Newfoundland Texts, (Department of Religious Studies, Memorial University of Newfoundland); available from (http://www.mun.ca/rels/hrollman/relsoc/texts/whitbourne/whititle.html).

3. John Mason, <u>A Briefe discourse of the New-found-land, 1620</u>, ed. by Dr. Hans Rollman, The Newfoundland and Labrador Pages: Newfoundland Texts, (Department of Religious Studies, Memorial University of Newfoundland); available from http://www.mun.ca/rels/hrollman/relsoc/texts/mason.html.

4. F.P. La Varenne, <u>The French Cook, Englished by I.D.G</u> (London: 1654).

5. D.W. Prowse, <u>A History of Newfoundland from English, Colonial and Foreign Records</u> (London: MacMillan and Co., 1895), 106.

6. Gervaise Markham, <u>The English Hous-wife</u> (London: 1656).

7. Elizabeth Cromwel, <u>The Court and Kitchin of Elizabeth</u> (London:1664).

8. <u>The Diary of Samuel Pepys</u>, ed. by Robert Latham and William Matthews, (Berkley: Univeristy of California Press, 1970), 2:.25.

9. "How to bear yourself at table" (Harl.Ms. 3362 fol.6) in <u>Manners and Meals in Olden Times</u>, ed. F.J. Furnivall (London: Trübner & Co., 1868), 27–29.

10. Markham.

11. Cell, <u>Newfoundland Discovered</u>, 201.

12. Markham.

13. Ibid.

◦ॐ Section ॐ◦

14. La Varenne.
15. "How to bear yourself at table", 27–29.
16. La Varenne.
17. Cell, <u>Newfoundland Discovered</u>, 201.
18. La Varenne.
19. Jay Anderson, "A Solid sufficiency: An Ethnography of Yeoman Foodways in Stuart England" (Phd. Thesis, University of Pennsylvannia, 1971), 240.
20. La Varenne.
21. Ibid.
22. Rebecca Price, <u>The Compleat Cook,</u> compiled by Madeleine Masson, (London: Routledge & Kegan Paul), 56.
23. Mason.
24. La Varenne.
25. Paul O'Neill, <u>The Oldest City, the Story of St. John's, Newfoundland</u> (Erin, Ontario: Press Porcepic, 1975), 45.
26. Ibid., 45.
27. La Varenne.
28. Ibid.
29. Markham.
30. La Varenne.
31. Sir Hugh Platt, <u>Delights for Ladies to adorne their persons, tables, closets and distillories</u> (London: 1611).
32. Markham.
33. Hannah Wolley, <u>The Accomplisht Ladies Delight</u> (London: 1686)
34. <u>The Journal of James Yonge 1647-1721, Plymouth Surgeon</u>, ed. by F. L.Poynter (London: Longmans, 1963), 132.
35. Cromwell.

Section

36. Lord P. Ruthuen, " The Art of courtship" in <u>The Ladies Cabinet Enlarged and opened</u> (London: 1654).

37. John Murrell, <u>A New Book of Cookerie</u> (London: 1615).

38. "How to bear yourself at table", 27–29.

39. E.Grey, <u>A True Gentlewomans Delight</u> (London: 1653).

40. H. Wolley, <u>The Queen-like Closet</u> (London: 1672).

41. Platt.

42. Cell, <u>Newfoundland Discovered</u>, 256.

43. Prowse, 129.

44. Patrick O'Flaherty, <u>Old Newfoundland: A History to 1843</u> (St. John's, NL: Long Beach Press, 1999), 34.

45. Prowse,127.

46. John Murrell, <u>A Delightful Daily Exercise</u> (London: 1623).

47. Andrew Boorde, <u>Compendyous Regyment or Dyetary of Health, 1542</u>, ed. F.J. Furnivall (London: Trübner & Co., 1870), 273.

48. Markham.

49. Gillian T. Cell, <u>English Enterprise in Newfoundland 1577-1660</u> (Toronto: University of Toronto Press, 1969), 77.

50. Markham.

51. Cell, <u>Newfoundland Discovered</u>, 245.

52. Markham.

53. Anderson, 101-102.

54. Markham.

55. Wolley, <u>The Accomplisht Ladies Delight.</u>

56. Sir John Harington, "The Preservation of Health, or a dyet for the Healthfull Man, 1624" in <u>Manners and Meals in Olden Times.</u> ed. by F.J. Furnivall, (London: Trübner & Co., 1868), 258.

57. C. Ann Wilson, <u>Food and Drink in Britain</u> (London: Constable, 1973), 193.

✼ Section ✼

58. Platt.
59. Whitbourne.
60. Markham.
61. Cell, Newfoundland Discovered, 201.
62. William Rabisha, The Whole Body of Cookery Dissected (London: 1661).
63. Prowse, 127.
64. Ruthuen.
65. Cell, Newfoundland Discovered, 74.
66. Ibid., 74.
67. Ibid., 74.
68. Ingeborg Marshall, *Reports and Letters by Christopher Pulling* (St. John's, NL: Breakwater Books, 1989), 125.
69. Whitbourne.
70. Mason.
71. Wilson, 311.
72. Ibid., 305.
73. Platt.
74. Ruthuen, "The Art of Courtship".
75. La Varenne.
76. Markham.
77. Robert May, The Accomplisht Cook (London: 1660).
78. Markham.
79. Ruthuen, The Ladies Cabinet Enlarged.
80. Paul O'Neill, The Oldest City, the Story of St. John's, Newfoundland (Erin, Ontario: Press Porcepic, 1975), 44.
81. Wilson, 288.

82. Wolley, The Queen-like Closet.

83. Platt.

84. Wilson, 245.

85. H. Wolley, The Compleat Cook (London: 1698).

86. Jane O'Hara-May, The Elizabethan Dyetary of Health (Kansas: Coronado Press, 1977), 172.

87. Platt.

88. Markham.

89. H. Wolley, The Queen-like Closet.

90. Cell, English Enterprise in Newfoundland, 65.

91. May.

92. Markham.

93. Temple Newsam, "The Gentlewoman's Kitchen" in A Taste of History, 10,000 years of Food in Britain (London: English Heritage, in association with British Museum Press, 1993), 203.

94. O'Hara-May, 172.

95. Markham.

96. "How to bear youself at table".

97. Ruthuen, The Ladies Cabinet Enlarged.

98. Platt.

99. Cell, English Enterprise in Newfoundland, 70.

100. O'Hara-May, 211.

101. Platt.

102. Wilson, 357.

103. Markham.

104. A.M. Lysaght, Joseph Banks in Newfoundland and Labrador (London: Faber and Faber Ltd., 1971), 139.

105. Markham.

⊗ Section ⊗

106. Platt.
107. Prowse, 154.
108. Ruthuen, The Ladies Cabinet Enlarged.
109. Kenelme Digbie, The Closet of the Eminently Learned Sir Kenelme Digbie (London:1669)
110. Murrell, A New Book of Cookerie.
111. Wolley, The Accomplisht Ladies Delight.
112. Platt.
113. William Vaughan, "William Vaughan's Fifteen Directions to preserve Health" in Manners and Meals in Olden Times, ed. by F.J. Furnivall (London: Trübner & Co., 1868), 249.
114. Wolley, The Queens Closet Opened (London: 1655).
115. Cell, Newfoundland Discovered, 80.
116. Wolley, The Queen's Closet Opened.
117. Ibid.
118. Markham.
119. Wolley. The Queens Closet Opened.
120. Elizabeth Grey, A Choice Manuall, or, Rare and Select Secrets in Physick and Chyrurgery (London: 1654).
121. O'Hara-May, 115.
122. Wolley. The Queens Closet Opened.
123. Ibid.
124. Harington, Sir John. "The Preservation of Health, or a dyet for the Healthfull Man" (London:1624.) in Manners and Meals in Olden Times, ed. F.J. Furnivall, (London: Trübner & Co., 1868), 257.
125. Grey, A Choice Manuell.
126. Harington, 259.
127. Grey, A Choice Manuall.

✐ Section ✑

128. Ibid.

129. Harington, 259.

130. Elizabeth Grey, A Choice Manuall.

131. Ibid.

132. Ibid.

133. Ruthuen. The Ladies Cabinet Enlarged.

134 Wolley, The Accomplisht Ladies Delight.

135. Ibid.

136. H. Wolley, The Queen-like Closet.

137. Prowse, 126.

138. Murrell, A Daily Exercise for Ladies.

139. Platt.

140. Cell, Newfoundland Discovered, 255.

Section

❦ Section ❧

Bibliography

Anderson, Jay. "A Solid sufficiency: An Ethnography of Yeoman Foodways in Stuart England." Phd. Thesis, University of Pennsylvannia, 1971.

Beeton, Mrs.Isabella Mary. <u>Mrs. Beeton's Cookery and Household Management</u>. London: 1861.

Boorde, A. <u>A Compendyous Regyment, or A Dyetary of Helth</u>. 1542, Edited by F.J. Furnivall. London: Trübner & Co., 1868.

Brears, Peter. <u>A Taste of History, 10,000 years of Food in Britain</u>. London: English Heritage, in association with British Museum Press, 1993.

Cell, Gillian T. <u>Newfoundland Discovered: English Attempts at Colonization 1610-1630</u>. London: Hakluyt Society, 1982.

Cell, Gillian T. <u>English Enterprise in Newfoundland 1577-1660</u>. Toronto: University of Toronto Press, 1969.

Crellin, J.K. (1999) "The Aire, in Newfoundland is Wholesome Good: The Medical Landscape of Newfoundland in the early Seventeenth-century". In <u>The Avalon Chronicles</u>, Vol. 4 (1999) : 1–24.

Crompton, Amanda J. "A 17th Century Planters House at Ferryland, Newfoundland (CgAf-2, Area D)" M.A. Thesis. Memorial University of Newfoundland, 2001.

Cromwel, Elizabeth. <u>The Court and Kitchin of Elizabeth</u>. London:1664.

Dawson, Thomas. <u>A Book of Cookery and the Order of Meats to be Served to the Table</u>. London: 1650.

Digbie, Kenelm. <u>The Closet of the Eminently Learned Sir Kenelme Digbie</u>. London:1669.

Early, Eleanor. <u>New England Cookbook</u>. New York:Random House, 1954.

"How to bear yourself at table" In <u>Manners and Meals in Olden Times</u>, Edited F.J. Furnivall. London: Trübner & Co., 1868.

145

☙ Section ❧

Gerard, John. The Herball or a General Historie of Plantes (1597). New York: Dover Publications, 1975.

Grey, Elizabeth. A Choice Manuall, or, Rare and Select Secrets in Physick and Chyrurgery. London: 1654.

Hale, William Harlan. The Horizon Cookbook and Illustrated History of Eating and Drinking through the Ages. New York: American Heritage Publishing Co., 1968.

Harding, Les. Historic St. John's. St. John's: Jesperson Press, 1993.

Harding, Les. Exploring the Avalon. St. John's: Jesperson Press, 1998.

Harington, Sir John. "The Preservation of Health, or a dyet for the Healthfull Man" London:1624. In Manners and Meals in Olden Times. Edited by F.J. Furnivall. London: Trübner & Co., 1868.

Latham, Robert and Matthews, William. The Diary of Samuel Pepys. Berkeley: University of California Press, 1970.

La Varenne, F.P. The French Cook (La Cuisinier Francois), Englished by I.D.G. London: 1654.

Leighton, Ann. Early American Gardens: for Meate or Medicine. Boston: Houghton Mifflin, 1979.

Lysaght, A.M. Joseph Banks in Newfoundland and Labrador. London: Faber and Faber Ltd., 1971.

Markham, Gervaise. The English Hous-wife. London: 1656.

Markham, Gervaise. The English Housewife. Edited by Michael R. Best. McGill-Queen's University Press, 1986.

Marshall, Ingeborg. A History and Ethnography of the Beothuk. Montreal: McGill-Queen's University Press, 1996.

Marshall, Ingeborg. Reports and Letters by Christopher Pulling. St. John's, NL: Breakwater Books, 1989.

Mason, John. A Briefe discourse of the New-found-land, 1620, ed. by Dr. Hans Rollman, The Newfoundland and Labrador Pages: Newfoundland Texts, (Department of Religious Studies, Memorial University of Newfoundland); available from http://www.mun.ca/rels/hrollman/relsoc/texts/mason.html.

⚘ Section ⚘

May, Robert. The Accomplisht Cook. London: 1660.

McCarthy, Michael. An Aspect of Newfoundland History: A History of Plaissance and Placentia 1501-1970. St. John's: 1973.

Murphy, Michael P. Pathways through Yesterday. St. John's: Town Crier Publishing Co., 1976.

Murrell, John. A Delightful Daily Exercise. London: 1623.

Murrell, John. A Daily Exercise for Ladies. London: 1617.

Murrell, John. A New Book of Cookerie. London: 1615.

O'Flaherty, Patrick. Old Newfoundland: a History to 1843. St. John's: Long Beach Press, 1999.

O'Hara-May, Jane. The Elizabethan Dyetary of Health. Kansas: Coronado Press, 1977

O'Neill, Paul. The Oldest City, the Story of St. John's, Newfoundland. Vol.1 Erin, Ontario: Press Porcepic, 1975.

Partridge, John. The Treasurie of Commodious Conceits and Hidden Secrets. London: 1573.

Platt, Sir Hugh. Delights for Ladies to adorne their persons, tables, closets and distillories, London: 1611.

Poole, Cyril F., Ed. Encyclopedia of Newfoundland and Labrador. St. John's: Harry Cuff Publications Ltd, 1994.

Pope, Dr. Peter. "The South Avalon Planters, 1630-1700: Residence, Labour, Demand and Exchange in Seventeenth-Century Newfoundland." St. John's: Ph.D. dissertation, Memorial University of Newfoundland, 1992.

Poynter, F.L., ed. The Journal of James Yonge 1647-1721, Plymouth Surgeon. London: Longmans, 1963.

Price Rebecca, The Compleat Cook compiled by Madeleine Masson. London: Routledge & Kegan Paul, 1974

Prowse, D.W. A History of Newfoundland from English, Colonial and Foreign Records. London: McMillan and Co.1895.

Quayle, Eric. Old Cook Books: An Illustrated History. New York: Dutton, 1978.

Quennell, M. and Quennell, C.H.B. A History of Everyday Things in England. London: C. Scribner's Sons, 1937.

Rabisha, William. The Whole Body of Cookery Dissected. London: 1661.

Roberts, Hugh D. Downhearth to Bar Grate. Wiltshire: Wiltshire Folk Life Society, 1981.

Rombauer, Irma S. and Rombauer Becker, Marion. Joy of Cooking. New York: The Bobbs-Merrill Company. Inc., 1988.

Ruthuen, Lord P. The Ladies Cabinet Enlarged and Opened. London: 1654.

Ruthuen, Lord P. "The Art of courtship", The Ladies Cabinet Enlarged and opened. London: 1654.

Seary, E.R. Place Names of the Avalon Peninsula of the Island of Newfoundland, Toronto: University of Toronto Press, 1971.

Scott, Peter. A Guide to the Gardens of Avalon, Ferryland, Newfoundland. St. John's: 1999.

Shirley, John. The Accomplished Ladies Rich Closet of Rarities. London: 1690.

Whitbourne, Richard. A Discourse and Discovery of New-found-land, 1620, ed. by Dr. Hans Rollman, The Newfoundland and Labrador Pages: Newfoundland Texts, (Department of Religious Studies, Memorial University of Newfoundland); available from (http://www.mun.ca/rels/hrollman/relsoc/texts/whitbourne/whititle.html)

Wilson, C. Ann. Food and Drink in Britain. London: Constable, 1973

Wolley, H. The Queen-like Closet. London: 1672.

Wolley, H. The Queens Closet Opened. London: 1674.

Wolley, H. The Accomplisht Ladies Delight. London: 1686.

Sheilah is a Newfoundlander, history lover, music teacher, singer and the mother of two teenagers, a cat and one large dog.